The Ultimate
Portuguese Cookbook

111 Dishes From Portugal To Cook Right Now

Slavka Bodic

Copyright @2020

All rights reserved. No part of this book may be reproduced in any form without writing permission in writing from the author. Reviewers may quote brief passages in reviews.

No part of this publication may be reproduced or transmitted in any form or by any means, mechanical or electronic, including photocopying or recording, or by any information storage and retrieval system, or transmitted by email without permission in writing from the publisher. While all attempts have been made to verify the information provided in this publication, neither the author nor the publisher assumes any responsibility for errors, omissions or contrary interpretations of the subject matter herein.

This book is for entertainment purposes only. The views expressed are those of the author alone and should not be taken as expert instruction or command. The reader is responsible for his or her actions. Adherence to all applicable laws and regulations, including international, federal, state and local governing professional licensing, business practices, advertising, and all other aspects of doing business in US, Canada or any other jurisdiction is the sole responsibility of the purchaser or reader.

Neither the author nor the publisher assumes any responsibility or liability whatsoever on the behalf of the purchaser or reader of these materials. Any perceived slight of any individual or organization is purely unintentional. Similarity with already published recipes is possible.

Imprint: Independently published

Please sign up for free Balkan and Mediterranean recipes:
www.balkanfood.org

Introduction

Since the 15th and 16th centuries, Portuguese cuisine has been renowned for its diverse and unique flavors and aromas. The culinary culture of Portugal has spread many influences around the world, whereas it's actually derived from the widespread Portuguese culture and its rich history. The great perk about Portuguese food is that it's amazingly tasty and also rich in nutritious ingredients like fresh vegetables and seafood. It offers a number of great combinations of vegetables, fruits, grains, beans, seafood, meats, etc. So if you're curious about Portuguese Cuisine and want to explore all its different flavors, then this cookbook is the perfect read for you. This cookbook is a gift for all those who are into unique European recipes and wants to give themselves a break from their routine menus. Now you can smell and taste authentic Portuguese meals at home using your basic kitchen ingredients, fresh vegetables, meats, and grains.

The Ultimate Portuguese Cookbook will introduce to Portuguese cuisine and its culinary culture in a way that you've likely never tried before. It brings you a variety of Portuguese recipes all in one place. The book is great for all those who are always keen to cook healthy food and want to explore its unique flavors. With the help of this Portuguese cuisine cookbook, you can create a complete Portuguese menu at home, or you can try all the special Portuguese recipes on your special occasions and festive celebrations. In this cookbook, you'll find popular Portuguese meals and the ones that you might not have heard of. From nourishing breakfast items to all of the soups, desserts, drinks, main dishes, and Portuguese salads, etc., you can find them all. And all these recipes are designed in such a simple way that those who aren't even familiar with the Portuguese culture, food, and language can still try and cook them at home without facing much difficulty.

Portuguese culinary culture and cuisine delights are full of surprises. You'll be amazed to know how the Portuguese left their influence on several other cuisines in the world. In this Portuguese cookbook, you'll find not only all the popular Portuguese but also a snippet about Portugal as a country and how it's worth exploring.

What you can find in this cookbook:
- Something about the Portuguese Cuisine
- Words About Portugal
- Portuguese Breakfast Recipes
- The Snacks, Sides, or Appetizers
- Main Dishes and Entrees
- Portuguese desserts and Drinks

Let's try all these Portuguese Recipes and recreate a complete menu to celebrate the amazing Portuguese flavors and mesmerizing aromas!

Table Of Contents

INTRODUCTION 3
WHY PORTUGUESE CUISINE? 9
PORTUGAL 11
BREAKFAST 13
    PORTUGUESE FRENCH TOAST (*RABANADAS*) 14
    PORTUGUESE CORNBREAD (*BROA*) 15
    PORTUGUESE RICE MUFFINS (*BOLOS DE ARROZ*) 17
    EGGS SCRAMBLED WITH SAUSAGE 19
    PORTUGUESE OMELET 21
    POTATO HASH WITH LINGUICA 23
    POTATO SAUSAGE FRITTATA 25
    PORTUGUESE BAKED EGGS 26
    ASPARAGUS AND CHORIZO OMELET 28
    PORTUGUESE BAKED OMELET 29
    STUFFED PORTUGUESE BREAD 30
    PORTUGUESE YOGURT BREAKFAST 32
    PORTUGUESE FIG JAM 33
    PORTUGUESE TUNA OMELET 34
APPETIZERS AND SNACKS 35
    PORTUGUESE SHRIMP PATTIES 36
    CHEESE HAM PATTIES 38
    MILHO FRITO 39
    FISH FOFO 40
    PORTUGUESE CHORIZO ROLLS 42
    LUPINI BEANS (*PORTUGUESE TREMOÇOS*) 43
    PORTUGUESE SHRIMP AND CHORIZO 44
    PORTUGUESE BEAN TARTS (*QUEIJADAS DE FEIJAO*) 46
    PORTUGUESE ROLL UPS 47
SALADS 48
    OCTOPUS SALAD (*SALADA DE POLVO*) 49
    BLACK EYED PEAS TUNA SALAD 50

Tuna Salad	51
Chicken and Peach Salad With Feta	52
Melon Cheese Salad	54
Portuguese Tomato Salad	55
Grilled Sardines Salad	56
Potato Vegetable Salad	57
Portuguese Chickpea Salad (Salada De Grao De Bico)	59
Portuguese Salad	60
Portuguese Watercress Salad	61

SOUPS 62

Portuguese Soup	63
Portuguese Bread Soup (Açorda Alentejana)	64
Portuguese Macaroni Bean Soup	65
Kale and Cabbage Soup	66
Traditional Fish Soup	68
Portuguese Bean Soup	70
Portuguese Chicken Soup	71
Tomato Soup with Eggs (Sopa de Tomate)	72

MAIN DISHES 73

Codfish with Cream	74
Portuguese Potato Cod Casserole (Bacalau)	76
Portuguese Pork Alentejana	78
Portuguese Steamed Clams	80
Shrimp Mozambique	81
Portuguese Sausage Kale Soup (Caldo Verde)	82
Portuguese Beef Stew	83
Seafood Bread Stew (Açorda de Marisco)	85
Portuguese Shrimps	86
Portuguese Rice (Arroz de Braga)	87
Green Cabbage (Caldo Verde)	89
Portuguese Beef Shish Kabobs (Espetadas)	90
Portuguese Rice and Beans (JAG)	91
Portuguese Beef Roast Sopas	92
Portuguese Style Beef Steaks	93
Portuguese Chicken	94
Wine Garlic Pork (Vina Dosh)	95

Portuguese Patty Melts 96
Portuguese Braised Chicken 98
Portuguese Stuffing Balls 99
Portuguese Rabbit 100
Chorizo Potato Stew 101
Pan-Fried Hake 102
Portuguese Grilled Lobsters 104
Portuguese Seafood Cataplana 105
One-Pot Chicken and Potatoes 106
Fisherman's Shrimp and Chorizo 108
Portuguese Mussels 110
Portuguese Prego Rolls 111
Piri-Piri Chicken with Potatoes 113
Piri-Piri Sauce 115
Chicken with Grapes 116
Garlicky Green Beans 118
Pickle Meat Stew (*Macao*) 119
Portuguese Fish Chowder 121
Seafood Rice 123
Fish Stew (*Caldeirada De Peixe*) 125
Portuguese Barbecued Pork (*Febras Assadas*) 127
Portuguese Prego With Piri-Piri 128
Grilled Portuguese Sardines 130
Piri-Piri Chicken with Winter Slaw 131

DESSERTS 133

Portuguese Sweet Rice 134
Portuguese Muffins (*Bolo Levedo*) 135
Portuguese Coconut Cakes (*Bolos de Coco*) 136
Portuguese Custard Tarts (*Pasteis de Nata*) 137
Serradura 139
Portuguese Doughnuts (*Bola De Berlim*) 140
Flan 142
Portuguese Bread (*Pão De Deus*) 144
Almond Carob Cake (*Tarte De Alfarroba E Amendôas*) 146
Egg White Soufflé (*Pudim Molotof*) 147
Orange Roll Cake 148
Brigadeiro Cake 149

CHOCOLATE MOUSSE..151
PORTUGUESE ALMOND CAKE (*TOUCINHO DO CÉU*)..152
CHOCOLATE SALAMI (*SALAME DE CHOCOLATE*) 153
PORTUGUESE VERMICELLI PUDDING (ALETRIA) 154
DRUNKEN PEARS 155
PUMPKIN DREAMS (*SONHOS DE ABÓBORA*) 156
WASHBOARD COOKIES (*LAVADORES*)..157
PORTUGUESE ALMOND CUPCAKES 158

DRINKS..159

CAPRIOSKA COCKTAIL 160
PORTO TONICO 161
PORTUGUESE DAISY 162
SOUR CHERRY LIQUEUR (*GINGINHA*) 163
PORTONIC 164
PORTUGUESE MARTINI 165
PORTUGUESE MORANGAO COCKTAIL 166
VINHO VERDE SANGRIA 167

ONE LAST THING 173

Why Portuguese Cuisine?

Portuguese cuisine is known for its diversity. Since the country is located on a peninsula and has a long coastline, the people there are very fond of seafood and eat a vast variety. There are several seafood recipes in Portuguese cuisine that you can enjoy, like the octopus's salad, fish stew, steamed mussels, and lobsters, etc. Perhaps, without seafood, the Portuguese cuisine is incomplete. Grilled sardines are also quite famous in Portugal. Soups and stews are also greatly enjoyed in this region. Whether it's the beef stew, sausage soup, or the chicken stew, you can have it all via the Portuguese food.

Due to Portugal's connection to mainland Europe and a Mediterranean country-Spain! The Portuguese cuisines make use of several of the Mediterranean ingredients like olives, cheese, and veggies. There are several other ingredients that are commonly used in traditional Portuguese meals like:

- Cinnamon
- Bell peppers
- Dates
- Feta cheese
- Olives
- Fish and seafood
- Pork, beef, and poultry
- Potatoes
- Kale
- Chili peppers

Portuguese dishes are known for their unique tastes and unforgettable aromas. There are several dishes that are worth trying on this cuisine, like:

- Portuguese Fish Chowder

- Seafood rice
- Fish Stew (*Caldeirada De Peixe*)
- Portuguese Barbecued Pork (*Febras Assadas)*
- Portuguese Prego With Piri-Piri
- Grilled Portuguese Sardines
- Piri-Piri Chicken with Winter Slaw

The popularly known Peri-Peri sauce is also inspired by Portuguese cuisine. Specifically, this sauce is used in several Portuguese recipes, whether to braise a roasting chicken or season the beef or pork. Amazing desserts can also be found in this cuisine, from cakes to doughnuts, chocolate salamis, and pumpkin bites. In fact, it was the Portuguese who first introduced the use of sugar and confectioneries to other parts of the world like Asia and South America, etc.

Portugal

Located in the southwestern European peninsula, Portugal or the Portuguese Republic is beloved for its amazing beaches and for Cristiano Ronaldo, of course! The country is present on the western-most side of mainland Europe, and it has the Atlantic Ocean on one side and borders with Spain on the other. Portugal is one of the oldest inhabited places in mainland Europe, and it was once ruled by many great civilizations like Greeks, Romans, Suebi, Germanic People, and Muslims. During the 15 and 16th centuries, Portugal has one of the biggest commercial and maritime empires in the world, which allowed its people to spread its culture and traditions to other places and regions in the world. This is the reason that Portuguese influence can still be observed in the cultures of several other countries like Brazil, the Middle Eastern counter, and some Asian regions like Macau. The Macanese Cuisine from this region closely resembles Portuguese cuisine. Today, there are more than 250 million individuals around the world who speak Portuguese, which reflects the massive impact of the Portuguese empire on the world.

Due to its rich Royal history, it has several amazing and mind-boggling architecture that reminds you of 16th century Portugal. Manueline is a Portuguese late Gothic which was designed and built using the traditional Portuguese style ornamentation. Lisbon holds many interesting sites that depict the soft Portuguese style architecture and the 18th-century Pombaline style. The places where I most enjoyed during my visit to Portugal included its wonderful beaches. Sagres is the iconic for picnics and a lovely spot to surf. Troia Peninsula gives you a stunning view from the Setubal castle if you ever get a chance to visit the place. Perhaps there are endless options for beach lovers when in Portugal, and each and every site is worth visiting at least once.

Besides its amazing beaches, visitors also grew fond of Portuguese culture and food. There were interesting similarities between Portuguese cuisine and other cuisines from around the world. For instance, the dish called Vindalho that's fairly popular in Goa, India, is a spicy curry that is, in fact, influenced by the Portuguese style of cooking as it involves the use of garlic, chili peppers, and vinegar.

The spices like cinnamon, which is widely using in Indian dishes, is a Portuguese imported spice. And the use of cinnamon is also quite popular in Portuguese recipes. The rice soup that is enjoyed in Asia as the Congee is also influenced by the Portuguese version of rice and chicken soup named the Canja. The soup was traditionally served to the ill and sick for quick healing. Beyond that, when the Portuguese traders reached Japan during the 1540s, they introduced refined sugar to the Japanese cuisine. The concept of confectioneries in Japanese cuisine didn't exist until the Portuguese traders arrived at their shores. So, a lot of new recipes became part of the Japanese cuisine under the influence of Portuguese like Sponge cake-Kasutera, Fios De Ovos-Angel hair, and the Konpeito-candy. Perhaps, Portugal, its culture, and food are highly interesting and worth exploring!

Breakfast

Portuguese French Toast (*Rabanadas*)

Preparation time: 15 minutes
Cook time: 6 minutes
Nutrition facts (per serving): 241 cal (17g fat, 12g protein, 1g fiber)

This Portuguese toast is one healthy breakfast that can be served with powdered sugar toppings, and you can practically prepare it in a few minutes. For that reason, they're also great to try even on weekday mornings.

Ingredients (4 servings)
1 cup of sugar
2 tablespoons ground cinnamon
4 large eggs
2 cups of milk
1 loaf (8 ounces) French bread, cut into slices
Oil for frying

Preparation
Mix 2 tablespoons of cinnamon with sugar in a small bowl. Beat the eggs with milk in a bowl. Set a skillet with 2 tablespoons oil over medium heat and dip the bread in the egg's mixture. Sear the bread toast in the oil for 3 minutes per side. Coat the bread with cinnamon sugar. Serve.

Portuguese Cornbread (*Broa*)

Preparation time: 10 minutes
Cook time: 30 minutes
Nutrition facts (per serving): 257 cal (4.2g fat, 6.5g protein, 3g fiber)

Let's have a rich and delicious, soft, moist, and crumbly cornbread on this Portuguese menu. Try it with breakfast and other entrees, and you'll simply love it.

Ingredients (8 servings)
1 cup milk
4 pats unsalted butter
2 teaspoons white sugar
1½ cups cornmeal
1 (¼ounce) package active dry yeast
1 pinch white sugar
¼ cup of warm water
3 cups all-purpose flour
1 teaspoon of sea salt
1 tablespoon olive oil

Preparation
Warm the milk in a suitable saucepan over medium heat and stir in the butter and 2 teaspoons of sugar Mix well, add cornmeal, and then mix well until smooth. Remove it from the heat and then allow it to cool. Mix the yeast with warm water and a pinch of sugar in a bowl. Leave the mixture for 5 minutes.

Mix the salt with flour in a bowl and add these ingredients to the yeast mixture, then mix well on low speed in a stand mixer until it forms dough. Add the milk mixture to the dough and continue mixing the dough. Grease a bowl and transfer the dough into it. Cover it with a plastic sheet, and then leave it for 2 hours.

Punch dough the dough and Divide the prepared dough into 2 boules. Place them on a baking sheet lined with a silicone mat. Leave the dough for 1 hour. Carve 4 crisscross slits on top of the dough. At 500 degrees F, preheat your oven and place a Dutch oven filled with water in the oven as it preheats. Bake the bread for 10 minutes in the preheated oven and reduce the heat to 400 degrees F and cook baking the bread for 20 minutes. Allow the bread to cool and then slice to serve.

Portuguese Rice Muffins (*Bolos de Arroz*)

Preparation time: 15 minutes
Cook time: 18 minutes
Nutrition facts (per serving): 256 cal (5.2g fat, 23g protein, 18g fiber)

Have you tried these muffins for breakfast? Well, here's a Portuguese recipe that gives you soft and delicious morning muffins in just a few minutes.

Ingredients (6 servings)
¾ cup granulated sugar
⅓ cup unsalted butter
2 ½ teaspoon baking powder
1 teaspoon lemon zest
Pinch salt
3 large eggs
½ cup milk
1 cup all-purpose flour
⅔ cup rice flour

Preparation
At 400 degrees F, preheat your oven. Place 6 paper cups on a baking sheet. Beat the milk, eggs, sugar, and butter in a bowl. Mix the flours with baking powder, salt, and lemon zest. Add this prepared mixture to the egg mixture and mix well until smooth. Divide the batter into the paper cups. Bake them for 18 minutes in the oven. Allow the muffins to cool. Serve.

Eggs Scrambled with Sausage

Preparation time: 15 minutes
Cook time: 6 minutes
Nutrition facts (per serving): 213 cal (20g fat, 9g protein, 7g fiber)

The Portuguese scramble is famous for its delicious flavor and the use of Portuguese sausage. Made from eggs, half and half, and cheese, this scramble pairs well with all types of toasted bread.

Ingredients (6 servings)
3 whole eggs
1 tablespoon half and half
1 tablespoon water
1 ounce Portuguese sausage chopped
2 green spring onions, chopped
¼ cup sharp cheddar cheese, shredded

Preparation
Beat the eggs with half and half and water in a small bowl. Sauté the sausage in a skillet for 3 minutes. Stir in the green onions and then sauté for almost 1 minute. Pour the egg mixture and cook for 1-2 minutes until set. Drizzle cheese on top and fold the eggs. Serve.

Portuguese Omelet

Preparation time: 10 minutes
Cook time: 33 minutes
Nutrition facts (per serving): 478 cal (16g fat, 14g protein, 2g fiber)

This Portuguese mushroom omelet tastes heavenly when cooked and baked at home using fresh ingredients. Serve warm with your favorite herbs and cheese toppings and toasted bread on the side.

Ingredients (12 servings)
1 cup yellow onion, chopped
12 large eggs
½ pound Cremini mushrooms, washed and sliced
1 pound ground pork
1 tablespoon garlic, minced
1 tablespoon dried oregano
1 teaspoon brown sugar
1 teaspoon allspice
1 teaspoon smoked paprika
1½ teaspoons liquid smoke
¼ cup dry red wine
1 tablespoon unsalted butter
Salt and black pepper to taste
Olive oil
Pinch of cayenne pepper

Preparation
Sauté the onion with oil in a sauté pan for 7 minutes. Stir in the garlic and sauté for almost 1 minute. Stir in the mushrooms and sauté for 10 minutes. Add the cayenne, paprika, allspice, brown sugar, liquid smoke, oregano, and pork, and then cook for 10 minutes. Stir in the red wine and cook until reduced to half. Stir in the butter, black pepper, and salt, and then mix well.

Make four wells in this prepared mixture and crack one egg into each well. Cover and cook for 5 minutes on low heat. Serve.

Potato Hash with Linguica

Preparation time: 15 minutes
Cook time: 12 minutes
Nutrition facts (per serving): 256 cal (16g fat, 9g protein, 6g fiber)

This potato hash is another nutritious yet simple meal for the breakfast table. It adds lots of nutrients and fibers to the table, along with healthy ingredients that are cooked together in a tempting combination.

Ingredients (8 servings)
½-pound linguiça sausage, diced
2 pounds russet potatoes, diced
1 yellow onion, diced
2 garlic cloves, minced
¾ cup canned garbanzo beans, drained
2 teaspoons sweet paprika
¾ teaspoon smoked paprika
1 ½ teaspoon salt
¼ teaspoon black pepper
¾ cup roasted red peppers, diced
⅓ cup green olives, halved
⅓ cup black olives, halved
4 large eggs
¼ cup parsley, chopped
Cooking oil for frying

Preparation
Sauté the linguica in a skillet until brown, then transfer to a plate while leaving the drippings in the skillet. Stir in the potatoes and sauté until golden brown. Transfer the potatoes to a plate. Add the oil and onions to the same skillet, then sauté until brown. Stir in the garlic and sauté for almost 30 seconds. Stir in the garbanzo beans and sauté for almost 1 minute.

Return the linguica and potatoes to the skillet, and then stir in the rest of the ingredients. Make four wells in this prepared mixture and crack one egg into each well. Transfer this skillet to the oven and bake for 10 minutes at 400 degrees F. Garnish with parsley. Serve.

Potato Sausage Frittata

Preparation time: 15 minutes
Cook time: 30 minutes
Nutrition facts (per serving): 410 cal (6g fat, 10g protein, 1.4g fiber)

Try this potato sausage frittata for your breakfast, and you'll forget about the rest. The recipe is simple and gives you lots of nutrients in one place.

Ingredients (8 servings)

3 tablespoons olive oil
½ pound Portuguese chorizo, sliced
2 garlic cloves, minced
¼ cup roasted red peppers, diced
7 large eggs
1 yellow onion, chopped
½ pound potatoes, peeled and sliced
Salt and black pepper, to taste
Chopped parsley leaves, for garnish

Preparation

Sauté the chorizo with 2 tablespoons oil in a skillet for 5 minutes, then transfer to a bowl. Add the potatoes, salt, black pepper, and onions to the same skillet, then sauté for 25 minutes. Stir in the garlic and sauté for almost 1 minute. Then transfer to a bowl with chorizo.

Beat the eggs with black pepper and salt in a bowl and pour over the chorizo mixture. Mix them gently. Add the remaining oil to a skillet and pour the mixture into the skillet. Finally, cook for almost 4 minutes. Slice and serve.

Portuguese Baked Eggs

Preparation time: 10 minutes
Cook time: 60 minutes
Nutrition facts (per serving): 591 cal (33g fat, 9g protein, 2g fiber)

Portuguese baked eggs are known as the classic Portuguese breakfast, which gives you all the right breakfast ingredients in one place- eggs, tomatoes, and bell peppers.

Ingredients (6 servings)
¼ cup olive oil
3 bell peppers, sliced
1 red onion, sliced
2 tomatoes, cut into wedges
8 garlic cloves, sliced
1 jalapeño, halved
¼ cup basil leaves
2 tablespoons oregano leaves
1 cup ricotta
6 large eggs
1 cup white cheddar, grated
1½ teaspoons chili powder
1 teaspoon paprika
¼ cup Parmesan, grated
Toasted country-style bread
Salt and black pepper, to taste

Preparation
Sauté the onion and bell peppers with oil in a large pot for 12 minutes. Stir in the paprika, chili powder, oregano, basil, jalapeno, garlic, and tomatoes, then sauté for 30 minutes. Stir in the black pepper and salt, and then discard the jalapeno.

At 400 degrees F, preheat the oven. Spread the bell pepper mixture in a 13x9 inches baking dish. Make 6 wells in the mixture and crack one egg into each well. Lastly, drizzle Parmesan and cheddar on top. Bake for 18 minutes.

Asparagus and Chorizo Omelet

Preparation time: 15 minutes
Cook time: 19 minutes
Nutrition facts (per serving): 226 cal (2.4g fat, 4g protein, 1g fiber)

This chorizo omelet is one of the Portuguese specialties, and it's best to have it with a different combination of cheeses and herbs toppings.

Ingredients (6 servings)
½ lbs. asparagus spears, cut into pieces
3 tablespoons olive oil
1 chorizo sausage, sliced
2 garlic cloves, chopped
5 eggs
2 onions, chopped
Salt and black pepper to taste

Preparation
Add the asparagus and water to a cooking pan and then cook for almost 4 minutes. Drain the asparagus and transfer to a suitable bowl. Sauté the onions with 2 tablespoons olive oil in a suitable saucepan for 7 minutes on low heat. Stir in the asparagus, garlic, and chorizo and sauté for 3 minutes. Beat all the eggs in a suitable bowl and pour over the asparagus mixture. Cook for 5 minutes per side. Slice and serve.

Portuguese Baked Omelet

Preparation time: 15 minutes
Cook time: 45 minutes
Nutrition facts (per serving): 471 cal (17g fat, 16g protein, 0.7g fiber)

This breakfast baked omelet is the best way to enjoy eggs in a savory style. It's a nice way to add broccoli, mushrooms, egg, ham, and cheese to your breakfast.

Ingredients (6 servings)
6 eggs
5 ounces mozzarella, minced
5 ounces ham, cubed
1 tomato, chopped and seeded
½ onion, chopped
5 tablespoons of milk
1 tablespoon of baking powder
3 tablespoons of flour
1 small can of mushrooms
1 cup of broccoli, chopped
Black pepper, to taste
Salt, to taste
Oregano, to taste

Preparation
At 350 degrees F, preheat your oven. Beat the eggs with baking powder, flour, and milk in a bowl. Stir in the broccoli, mushrooms, oregano, mozzarella, ham, tomato, onion, black pepper, and salt. Mix well and spread this prepared mixture in a greased pan. Bake the omelet for 45 minutes. Slice and serve.

Stuffed Portuguese Bread

Preparation time: 10 minutes
Cook time: 40 minutes
Nutrition facts (per serving): 317 cal (14g fat, 8.9g protein, 0.3g fiber)

The stuffed Portuguese bread has to parallel. This stuffed bread is super crispy on the outside and stuffed with cheesy bell pepper fillings on the inside.

Ingredients (6 servings)
4 teaspoons yeast
½ cup warm water
2 cups wheat flour
1 ½ tablespoon sugar
1 egg
3 ½ tablespoon oil
4 tablespoons tomato paste
1 green pepper, cut into strips
½ yellow pepper, cut into strips
2 ¼ cups mozzarella cheese
3 hard-boiled eggs
2 tablespoons oregano
1 egg yolk, beaten
Salt, to taste

Preparation
Mix the water with yeast, sugar, and 1 cup of sugar in a medium bowl. Leave it for 20 minutes. Stir in the oil, 1 egg, salt, and remaining flour. Mix well and knead for 15 minutes. Cover the prepared dough and leave for 30 minutes.

Roll the dough in a large circle, larger than the Bundt pan diameter. Place the dough in the pan with its edges hanging outside. Cut a small circle at the center of the pan. Brush the dough with tomato paste, and then add the peppers, mozzarella, oregano, and boiled eggs on top. Fold the hanging edges over the filling. Brush the dough with egg yolk and bake for 40 minutes at 350 degrees F. Serve warm.

Portuguese Yogurt Breakfast

Preparation time: 15 minutes
Nutrition facts (per serving): 242 cal (8.4g fat, 5.2g protein, 1g fiber)

If you haven't tried this Portuguese yogurt breakfast before, then here comes an authentic, simple, and easy to cook recipe that you can prepare at home in no time with minimum efforts.

Ingredients (6 servings)
1 cup plain yogurt
4 tablespoons corn flakes
1 ½ papayas, sliced
1 tablespoon linseeds
1 teaspoon honey

Preparation
Beat the yogurt with honey in a bowl. Top the yogurt with cornflakes, seeds, and papayas. Serve.

Portuguese Fig Jam

Preparation time: 5 minutes
Cook time: 10 minutes
Nutrition facts (per serving): 231 cal (20g fat, 22g protein, 6g fiber)

This fig jam is a must to have for every breakfast table. It's served with toasted bread, bagels, and buns.

Ingredients (12 servings)
1 ½ lb. of figs
2 ½ cups sugar
Juice of 1 orange
1 shot of Port wine
1 cinnamon stick

Preparation
Mix the port wine, figs, sugar, cinnamon stick, and orange juice in a suitable saucepan and cook until the mixture boils. Reduce the heat and cook until figs are soft. Mix well and allow it to cool. Serve.

Portuguese Tuna Omelet

Preparation time: 15 minutes
Cook time: 15 minutes
Nutrition facts (per serving): 230 cal (4.2g fat, 10g protein, 1.4g fiber)

If you haven't tried the Portuguese tuna omelet before, then here comes an authentic, simple, and easy to cook recipe that you can easily prepare and cook at home in no time with minimum efforts.

Ingredients (4 servings)
4 eggs
1 large can of tuna
2 small tomatoes, chopped
½ cup of heavy cream
½ onion, chopped
2 tablespoons of parsley, chopped
Olive oil, to taste
Salt and pepper, to taste
Grated cheese, to taste

Preparation
At 350 degrees F, preheat your oven. Beat the eggs with all the ingredients, except the oil. Spread this prepared mixture in a greased pan and top it with cheese. Bake for 15 minutes, and then slice. Serve.

Appetizers and Snacks

Portuguese Shrimp Patties

Preparation time: 10 minutes
Cook time: 15 minutes
Nutrition facts (per serving): 162 cal (13g fat, 7.5g protein, 2g fiber)

If you can't think of anything to cook and make in a short time, then try these Portuguese shrimp patties appetizer because it has great taste and texture to serve at the table.

Ingredients (8 servings)
Batter
2 cups of flour
2 ¾ cups of water
½ cup of margarine
Peel from 1 lemon
Coarse salt, to taste

Filling
2 lbs. of shrimp
4 cups of water
1 chopped onion
½ cup of margarine
½ cup of flour
1 tablespoon of tomato paste
3 eggs
1 cup of milk
Chopped parsley, to taste
Half lemon
Black pepper, to taste
Salt, to taste
Nutmeg, to taste
Breadcrumbs, to taste

Flour for sprinkling
Cooking oil, for frying

Preparation
Boil 4 cups water with salt in a suitable saucepan. Next, stir in the shrimp and cook for 3 minutes. Drain the shrimp, peel, and chop ten shrimp. Sauté the onion with margarine in a pan until brown. Stir in the flour, milk, and shrimp broth and then mix well. Stir in the chopped shrimp and tomato paste. Mix well and then add the nutmeg, black pepper, lemon juice, remaining shrimp, and chopped parsley. Then cook until it bubbles.

Mix the water with salt, lemon peel, and margarine in a pan. Cook until the mixture boils, stir in flour, and then mix well. Remove the pan from the heat. Divide the prepared dough in half and spread each into a sheet. Spread the shrimp mixture on top of one sheet and place the other dough sheet on top. Press the rim of a glass cup over the dough to cut out round patties. Dip each patty in eggs and coat it with breadcrumbs. Deep fry the prepared patties in hot oil until golden brown. Serve.

Cheese Ham Patties

Preparation time: 15 minutes
Cook time: 20 minutes
Nutrition facts (per serving): 106 cal (9g fat, 4g protein, 0.1g fiber)

The appetizing cheese ham patties make a great addition to the menu, and they look fantastic when served at the table.

Ingredients (6 servings)
Dough
1 cup of flour
1 cup of water
1 tablespoon margarine
Salt, to taste

Filling
¾ lb. of cheese
¾ lb. of ham
½ cup of black olives

Coating
1 egg, beaten
Breadcrumbs, to coat

Preparation
Mix the water with salt, water, and margarine in a pan. Cook until the mixture boils, then stir in flour, then mix well. Remove the pan from the heat. Divide the prepared dough in half and spread each into a sheet. Add the chopped cheese, ham, and olives over one dough sheet and place the other dough sheet on top. Press the rim of a glass cup over the dough to cut out round patties. Dip each patty in eggs and coat it with breadcrumbs. Deep fry the prepared patties in hot oil until golden brown. Serve.

Milho Frito

Preparation time: 15 minutes
Cook time: 2 hours 15 minutes
Nutrition facts (per serving): 79 cal (5.2g fat, 2.8g protein, 3g fiber)

If you haven't tried the crispy Milho Frito, then you must as they have no parallel in taste and texture.

Ingredients (6 servings)
3 tablespoons lard
4 garlic cloves, chopped
1 tablespoon thyme and mint, chopped
4 ⅓ cups white masa Harina
½ teaspoons fresh malagueta, minced
2 ½ teaspoons salt
Olive oil for greasing
Vegetable oil for frying

Preparation
Sauté the garlic with lard in a pan for 4 minutes. Stir in the 10 cups water and cook to a boil. Stir in the herbs, masa, salt, and malagueta. Mix well and cook on a boil, then reduce the heat. Cook for 2 hours with occasional stirring. Grease a 9x13 inches baking dish with olive oil. Spread the masa mixture in the baking dish. Cover and refrigerate the dish overnight.

Slice the Frito into cubes. Add the oil to a deep-frying pan and heat it to 350 degrees F. Deep fry the masa cubes until golden. Transfer to a plate lined with a paper towel. Serve.

Fish Fofo

Preparation time: 15 minutes
Cook time: 20 minutes
Nutrition facts (per serving): 124 cal (4.8g fat, 9.7g protein, 0.9g fiber)

If you want some new flavors in your meals, then this fish Fofo recipe is best to bring variety to the menu.

Ingredients (15 servings)
21 ounces (600 g) skinless haddock
10 ½ ounces boiled potatoes, grated
1 green birds-eye chili, chopped
3 tablespoons coriander leaves chopped
1 teaspoon cumin seeds, ground
½ teaspoons black peppercorns, ground
3 garlic cloves, chopped
2 thumb-sized ginger pieces, chopped
2 tablespoons rice flour
3 eggs
¼ cup dried breadcrumbs
Vegetable oil for frying

Preparation
Boil the fish in salted water in a suitable saucepan for 10 minutes. Then drain and transfer to a suitable bowl. Flake the fish into a piece, then add the potatoes, ginger, garlic, black pepper, cumin, coriander, and green chili, then mix well. Make 15 small logs from this prepared mixture. Beat the eggs in one bowl and spread breadcrumbs in another bowl.

Dip the potato balls in the eggs and coat them with breadcrumbs. Place them on a baking sheet and refrigerate for 1 hour. Heat the oil for deep frying in a pot over medium heat and deep fry the fofos for at least 2 minutes per side until golden brown. Transfer the fofos to a plate lined with a paper towel using a slotted spoon. Serve warm.

Portuguese Chorizo Rolls

Preparation time: 10 minutes
Cook time: 20 minutes
Nutrition facts (per serving): 231 cal (9.5g fat, 9.7g protein, 9g fiber)

Who doesn't like stuffed bread rolls? Well, here comes a bread roll stuffed with delicious chorizo to serve at the snack table.

Ingredients (2 servings)
2 teaspoons active dry yeast
1 cup tepid water
2 teaspoons sugar
1 tablespoon olive oil
3 ¾ cups bread flour
1 teaspoon salt
10 ounces cooked chorizo

Preparation
Mix warm water, 2 tsps. of yeast, and sugar in a suitable bowl and leave it for 10 minutes. Add the olive oil, flour, and salt, then mix well for 5 minutes, and then knead for 10 minutes. Transfer the dough to a greased pan, cover with a cling film and leave it for 2 hours.

At 450 degrees F, preheat your oven. Divide the prepared dough into 4 pieces and spread each dough into 6 inches round. Cut the chorizo into 12 pieces and place 3 slices over each dough round and fold the dough over the chorizo. Place the wrapped chorizo on a baking sheet and bake for 20 minutes in the oven. Serve warm.

Lupini Beans (*Portuguese Tremoços*)

Preparation time: 15 minutes
Cook time: 50 minutes
Nutrition facts (per serving): 232 cal (11g fat, 13g protein, 3g fiber)

The Lupini beans make a healthy meal for the table. The recipe to cook these beans is quite simple, with minimum ingredients used.

Ingredients (6 servings)
10 ½ ounces uncooked Lupini beans
4 garlic cloves, minced
1 tablespoon salt
Water
Olives

Preparation
Add water and Lupini beans to a cooking pot and cook for 50 minutes. Drain the beans and rinse the beans under the clean water. Soak the beans in a jar full of water, seal the lid, and leave it for 7 days. Drain and mix the beans with garlic, salt, and olives in a bowl. Serve.

Portuguese Shrimp and Chorizo

Preparation time: 15 minutes
Cook time: 7 minutes
Nutrition facts (per serving): 196 cal (3g fat, 12g protein, 3g fiber)

Portuguese shrimp with chorizo is another Portuguese delight that you should definitely try on this cuisine. Serve with a flavorsome sauce.

Ingredients (6 servings)

10 ½ ounces large shrimp
2 ounces Chorizo sausage, sliced
1 garlic clove, minced
2 green onion whites, cut into fine rounds
¼ ounce cilantro, chopped
9 grape tomatoes halved
5 black olives halved
1 bay leaf
½ teaspoon paprika
1 pinch chili flakes
⅛ cup white wine
1 tablespoon olive oil
1 pinch of salt and white pepper
¼ ounce melted butter

Preparation

Sauté the oil with chorizo in a skillet until brown. Stir in the green onion, then sauté for almost 1 minute. Stir in the cilantro, garlic, chili flakes, bay leaf, and paprika. Sauté for almost 1 minute. Stir in the tomatoes and wine, and then cook for 1 minute.

Stir in the shrimp, cover, and cook for almost 4 minutes. Mix well and then remove the shrimp from the heat. Stir in the cilantro, olives, and butter. Toss well and serve.

Portuguese Bean Tarts (*Queijadas De Feijao*)

Preparation time: 10 minutes
Cook time: 45 minutes
Nutrition facts (per serving): 101 cal (3g fat, 14g protein, 4g fiber)

What about a delicious bean tart? If you haven't tried these tarts before, now is the time to cook this delicious mix at home using simple and healthy ingredients.

Ingredients (12 servings)
12 eggs, separated
2 cans beans, drained and mashed
2 cups of sugar
2 tablespoons margarine
Water

Preparation
Mix water and sugar in a suitable saucepan on medium heat until caramelized. Stir in the beans and margarine, and then mix well. Allow the prepared mixture to cool, then whisk in 12 yolks and beat well. Stir in the 2 egg whites. Divide the prepared batter into the muffin cups and bake for 45 minutes at 350 degrees F. Garnish with sugar and serve.

Portuguese Roll-Ups

Preparation time: 10 minutes
Cook time: 10 minutes
Nutrition facts (per serving): 278 cal (21g fat, 9g protein, 3.1g fiber)

This is perhaps the simplest snack recipe from this cookbook. All you need to do is wrap the dates with bacon and bake to serve a crispy yet sweet delight.

Ingredients (15 servings)
1-pound bacon strips, sliced in half
30 dates

Preparation
Place one date on top of each bacon slice and wrap it around. Secure the wrap with a toothpick. Set the wrapped dates on a baking sheet and broil them for 10 minutes a 400 degrees F in the oven. Serve.

Salads

Octopus Salad (*Salada De Polvo*)

Preparation time: 15 minutes
Cook time: 50 minutes
Nutrition facts (per serving): 346 cal (14g fat, 3g protein, 4g fiber)

This octopus salad is quite popular in Portugal, and people who are looking for a recipe to try octopus on their menu can definitely make an introduction with this recipe.

Ingredients (6 servings)
3 lbs. octopus
8 peppercorns
1 white onion, quartered
1 carrot in chunks
3 garlic cloves
1 bunch cilantro stems
1 red bell pepper roasted and chopped
½ cup sun-dried tomatoes
1 red onion chopped
1 bunch cilantro leaves, chopped
1 lime juice of
¼ cup olive oil
Salt and black pepper to taste

Preparation
Add the octopus, carrot, garlic; white onion, peppercorns, cilantro stems to a saucepan. Pour in enough water to cover the veggies. Cook the mixture to a boil, then drain. Transfer the octopus to a pan filled with water and soak for 5 minutes. Transfer the pan to heat and cook for 50 minutes. Drain and chop the octopus. Transfer the octopus and the rest of the ingredients to a salad bowl. Toss well and serve.

Black-Eyed Peas Tuna Salad

Preparation time: 10 minutes
Nutrition facts (per serving): 72 cal (5g fat, 1.4g protein, 2g fiber)

The black-eyed peas tuna salad makes a great side serving for the table, and you can serve them a delicious and healthy snack meal as well.

Ingredients (6 servings)
1 ½ cup black-eyed peas, boiled
5 tablespoons olive oil
3 tablespoons white wine vinegar
1 small yellow onion, sliced
2 small garlic cloves, minced
4 tablespoons parsley leaves, sliced
9 ounces canned tuna in oil, drained and flaked
Salt and black pepper, to taste

Preparation
Add the black-eyed peas, olive oil, wine vinegar, onion, garlic, parsley, tuna, salt, and black pepper to a salad bowl. Mix well and serve.

Tuna Salad

Preparation time: 10 minutes
Cook time: 20 minutes
Nutrition facts (per serving): 56 cal (3.5g fat, 5.7g protein, 2g fiber)

This tuna salad is another most popular salad in Portuguese cuisine, and it has this amazing taste that it takes from the mix of chickpeas and olives.

Ingredients (4 servings)
1 (15-ounces) can chickpeas, drained
1 ½ lb. potatoes, cut into pieces
4 hard-boiled eggs, quartered
½ red onion, diced
⅓ cup Kalamata olives in oil, drained
12 ounces canned tuna
2 tablespoons olive oil
2 tablespoons red wine vinegar
Sea salt, to taste
Black pepper, to taste

Preparation
Boil salted water in a large suitable pot and add the potatoes. Cook until the potatoes are soft, then drain, then transfer to a bowl. Stir in the chickpeas, onion, olives, tuna, olive oil, vinegar, black pepper, salt, and eggs. Mix well and serve.

Chicken and Peach Salad With Feta

Preparation time: 10 minutes
Cook time: 43 minutes
Nutrition facts (per serving): 211 cal (20g fat, 4g protein, 13g fiber)

The chicken, peach, and feta salad offers the right fit to serve with all your Portuguese entrees. Here the crispy chicken is mixed with veggies and peaches for a wholesome flavor.

Ingredients (8 servings)
4 pounds whole chicken
¼ cup olive oil
2 garlic cloves, crushed
1 lemon, juiced
¼ cup Portuguese chicken seasoning
1 tablespoon dried oregano leaves
Spray olive oil
4 ripe peaches, halved, cut into wedges
3 ½ ounces Coles Brand mesclun mix
3 ½ ounces feta, crumbled
1 red onion, sliced
10 ⅔ ounces tomato Medley, halved
⅓ cup mint leaves

Dressing
¼ cup olive oil
2 tablespoons balsamic vinegar
1 teaspoon Brand honey

Preparation
Mix the oregano, seasoning, lemon juice, garlic, and oil in a small bowl. Rub this prepared mixture over the chicken, place the chicken in a glass dish, and

cover to refrigerate for 1 hour. Toss the peach wedges with oil in a pan and sauté for 3 minutes.

At 390 degrees F, preheat your oven. Bake the chicken for almost 40 minutes and flip the chicken once cooked halfway through. Cut the baked chicken into pieces. Toss the remaining ingredients with sautéed peaches in a salad bowl. Garnish with chicken. Serve.

Melon Cheese Salad

Preparation time: 10 minutes
Nutrition facts (per serving): 253 cal (2g fat, 21g protein, 4g fiber)

Melon cheese salad is a delicious and healthy salad, which has a refreshing taste due to the use of olive and lettuce in it.

Ingredients (6 servings)
1 ½ ounce black olives
½ bulb fennel chopped
½ large melon, sliced
1 bunch of chopped lettuce
1 chopped red pepper
5 ounces fresh cheese, shredded
8 tablespoons olive oil
3 tablespoons balsamic vinegar
3 chopped basil leaves
Salt and black pepper to taste

Preparation
Toss all the melon cheese salad ingredients in a salad bowl. Serve.

Portuguese Tomato Salad

Preparation time: 10 minutes
Nutrition facts (per serving): 179 cal (16g fat, 5g protein, 3g fiber)

Portuguese tomato salad is a special veggie salad, and it's a staple to accompany all the different entrees. Use this quick and simple recipe to get it ready in no time.

Ingredients (6 servings)
6 ripe tomatoes, diced
½ cup white onion, sliced
⅓ cup olive oil
¼ cup red wine vinegar
Salt and black pepper, to taste
1 handful parsley leaves, chopped
1 handful cilantro leaves, chopped

Preparation
Toss all the Portuguese tomato salad ingredients in a salad bowl. Serve.

Grilled Sardines Salad

Preparation time: 10 minutes
Cook time: 31 minutes
Nutrition facts (per serving): 176 cal (17g fat, 7g protein, 3g fiber)

It's as if the Portuguese menu is incomplete without some sardines in it. So here comes a sardine salad, which is made from potatoes, tomatoes, and sardines.

Ingredients (4 servings)
2 potatoes, peeled, boiled, and diced
1 tablespoon hot smoked paprika
¼ cup olive oil
1 red bell pepper
1 yellow bell pepper
2 tomatoes, chopped
1 red onion, halved, sliced
1 handful of coriander sprigs
1 teaspoon lemon juice
8 fresh sardines, cleaned
1 lemon, quartered

Preparation
Toss the boiled potatoes with 1 tablespoon oil and paprika on a baking sheet and bake them for almost 20 minutes in the oven at 350 degrees F. Prepare a grill over medium-high heat. Grease its grill with oil, grill the bell peppers for 5 minutes per side, and then transfer to a plate. Chop the bell peppers. Toss the potatoes with black pepper, salt, 2 tablespoons oil, lemon juice, coriander, onion, and tomatoes to a salad bowl. Toss well. Grill the sardines in the hot grill for 3 minutes per side. Place the sardines on top of the salad. Garnish with lemon and serve.

Potato Vegetable Salad

Preparation time: 10 minutes
Cook time: 35 minutes
Nutrition facts (per serving): 155 cal (8g fat, 13g protein, 2g fiber)

If you haven't tried the potato vegetable salad before, then here comes an authentic, simple, and easy to cook recipe that you can recreate easily at home in minimum time.

Ingredients (6 servings)
Salad
5 carrots peeled and cut into thirds
5 Yukon potatoes, peeled and quartered
1 yellow onion, peeled and quartered
½ head rapini, chopped
4 large eggs
3 garlic cloves, minced
1-2 dried bay leaves
½ tablespoon olive oil
¼ teaspoon sea salt

Dressing
⅓ cup olive oil
¼ cup parsley chopped
1 garlic clove minced
1 tablespoon red wine vinegar
1 teaspoon Dijon mustard
¼ teaspoon paprika
1 pinch sea salt
1 pinch black pepper

Preparation

Add the potatoes, carrots, olive oil, bay leaves, garlic, onion, a pinch of salt, and carrots to a saucepan and fill it with enough water to cover. Cook the veggies for 25 minutes. Add the rapini and eggs to a pan after 10 minutes. Drain and transfer the boiled eggs to a bowl, and veggies and the rest of the ingredients to a salad bowl. Peel the eggs and dice them. Add the diced eggs to the salad bowl. Whisk the dressing ingredients in a bowl and pour them into the salad. Toss well and serve.

Portuguese Chickpea Salad
(*Salada De Grao De Bico*)

Preparation time: 10 minutes
Nutrition facts (per serving): 243 cal (9g fat, 9g protein, 8g fiber)

Portuguese chickpeas salad has an amazing taste and a nutritious mix of chickpeas with veggies. Serve it with all types of entrees.

Ingredients (4 servings)
30 ounces chickpeas
¼ cup yellow onion, diced
¾ cup red bell pepper, diced
1 garlic clove, chopped
½ cup fresh parsley, chopped
¼ cup olive oil
3 tablespoons red wine vinegar
Salt and black pepper to taste

Preparation
Toss all the chickpea salad ingredients in a salad bowl. Serve.

Portuguese Salad

Preparation time: 15 minutes
Nutrition facts (per serving): 181 cal (5g fat, 7g protein, 6g fiber)

If you haven't tried this Portuguese bell pepper salad before, then here comes an authentic, simple, and easy to cook recipe that you can swiftly prepare yourself.

Ingredients (4 servings)
1 red bell pepper, chopped
1 green bell pepper, chopped
3 plum tomatoes, chopped
¼ cup olive oil
1 cucumber, peeled and chopped
¼ cup cilantro, chopped
2 tablespoons red wine vinegar
1 teaspoon chili paste
Salt and black pepper, to taste

Preparation
Toss all the Portuguese salad ingredients in a salad bowl. Serve.

Portuguese Watercress Salad

Preparation time: 15 minutes
Nutrition facts (per serving): 312 cal (16g fat, 13g protein, 1g fiber)

The Portuguese watercress salad is a delight to serve with every entree. It's known for its lemon vinaigrette and refreshing taste.

Ingredients (6 servings)
Vinaigrette
¼ cup fresh lemon juice
1 tablespoon red wine vinegar
2 garlic cloves, minced
½ teaspoons salt
½ teaspoons black pepper
¼ cup olive oil

Salad
6 cups romaine lettuce, chopped
6 cups watercress, stems trimmed
2 cups cucumber peeled, halved, and sliced
1 cup red onion, sliced
1 cup red bell pepper, diced
½ cup pimento-stuffed green olives halved

Preparation
Toss all the ingredients for the vinaigrette in a salad bowl. Add the rest of the ingredients, and then mix well. Serve.

Soups

Portuguese Soup

Preparation time: 10 minutes
Cook time: 1 hour 40 minutes
Nutrition facts (per serving): 537 cal (20g fat, 21g protein, 4g fiber)

Enjoy this Portuguese soup with potatoes and cabbage flavors. Adding kidney beans to the soup delivers a very strong taste to all the herbs and spices.

Ingredients (6 servings)
¼ cup of vegetable oil
2 cups onion, chopped
1-pound smoked sausage, sliced
1 medium head cabbage, chopped
6 potatoes, peeled and cubed
2 (15 ounce) cans kidney beans
2 cups ketchup
1 (10 ½ ounce) can beef consommé
2 ⅔ quarts water
2 teaspoons garlic powder
2 teaspoons black pepper
1 teaspoon salt
½ cup vinegar

Preparation
Sauté the onions with oil in a large pot over medium heat for 5 minutes. Add sausage and sauté for 5 minutes. Stir in the water, consommé, ketchup, beans, potatoes, cabbage, salt, black pepper, and garlic powder. Cook the mixture to a boil, reduce the heat and cook on a simmer for 30 minutes. Add the vinegar and cook for 1 hour on a simmer. If the mixture is too thick, add some water. Serve warm.

Portuguese Bread Soup (*Açorda Alentejana*)

Preparation time: 10 minutes
Cook time: 1 hour 10 minutes
Nutrition facts (per serving): 396 cal (13g fat, 12g protein, 4g fiber)

This bread soup is simply loved by all, the old and the young, and as it makes a healthy meal. Try this recipe at home.

Ingredients (6 servings)
1 lb. sturdy rustic-style bread, cut into 2-inch chunks
4 garlic cloves, peeled
1 bunch cilantro, washed and chopped
½ teaspoon salt
6 cups of water
4 eggs
4 tablespoons olive oil
Black pepper, to taste

Preparation
Spread the bread chunks on a baking sheet and bake for 1 hour at 250 degrees F. Blend ½ teaspoons salt, cilantro, and garlic in a blender until smooth. Boil water in a suitable saucepan and crack the eggs into the water one at a time until the eggs are poached. Pour the water into the cilantro paste, and then mix well. Stir in the oil and bread cubes, mix, and soak them for 5 minutes. Add salt for seasoning. Garnish with poached eggs and serve.

Portuguese Macaroni Bean Soup

Preparation time: 15 minutes
Cook time: 2 hours 10 minutes
Nutrition facts (per serving): 573 cal (31g fat, 29g protein, 7g fiber)

A perfect mix of Portuguese sausages, cabbage, macaroni, beans, and ham, this soup recipe is a warming bliss for all. Serve warm with your favorite bread.

Ingredients (6 servings)
2 pounds spicy Portuguese sausage, sliced
1-pound ham hocks
1 onion, sliced
2 quarts water
2 carrots, diced
3 potatoes, diced
1 small head cabbage, chopped
1 (8 ounces) can tomato sauce
2 (15 ounce) cans kidney beans
1 (16 ounces) package of macaroni

Preparation
Add water, onion, ham hocks, and sausage to a large pot, cover, and cook for 1 hour on a simmer. Then remove the ham from the soup and cut it into pieces. Return the ham hock to the pot. Add the tomato sauce, cabbage, potatoes, and carrots, cover, and cook for 60 minutes. Add the pasta and beans, and then cook for 10 minutes. Serve warm.

Kale and Cabbage Soup

Preparation time: 10 minutes
Cook time: 65 minutes
Nutrition facts (per serving): 199 cal (7.9g fat, 11g protein, 2.4g fiber)

This classic soup is here to make your meal special. You can always serve the soup with your favorite side meal.

Ingredients (8 servings)
4 tomatoes, peeled and chopped
1 tablespoon butter
1 tablespoon dried minced onion
Salt and black pepper to taste
2 tablespoons olive oil
4 celery stalks, chopped
1 onion, chopped
3 garlic cloves, minced
2 bay leaves
8 cups hot water
½ head green cabbage, shredded
½ cup beef base
1 teaspoon Herbes de Provence
1 pinch red pepper flakes
1 (15 ounces) can kidney beans, drained
1 bunch kale, chopped

Preparation
Add black pepper, salt, onion, butter, and tomatoes to a saucepan and cook over medium heat for 15 minutes. Sauté the onion, bay leaves, and garlic with olive oil in a stockpot for 5 minutes over medium heat. Stir in the cooked tomato mixture and cook for 5 minutes. Discard the bay leaves and add water, green cabbage, and red pepper flakes, Herbes de Provence, and

beef base. Cover partially and cook for 25 minutes. Add kale and kidney beans and cover again to cook for 15 minutes. Serve warm.

Traditional Fish Soup

Preparation time: 15 minutes
Cook time: 21 minutes
Nutrition facts (per serving): 53 cal (31g fat, 101g protein, 2g fiber)

This fish soup tastes amazing, and it simple and easy to cook. It's great for all seafood lovers and is best served during winter.

Ingredients (6 servings)
4 boneless shark fish chunks
1 bunch fresh oregano
1 bay leaf
Rustic bread, sliced
Sweet paprika, to taste
Salt, to taste
4 garlic cloves, sliced
¼ cup white wine vinegar
1 tablespoon plain flour
½ cup olive oil
2 cups of water
Black pepper, to taste
1 egg, beaten
1 onion, chopped
½ green pepper, chopped
1 tablespoon tomato paste
1 fish stock cube

Preparation
Mix ½ teaspoons paprika, bay leaf, 3 tablespoons of olive oil and vinegar in a bowl with the fish pieces. Mix well, cover and marinate for almost 2 hours. Sauté the onion, green pepper and garlic with olive oil in a pan for 6 minutes. Stir in the water, fish with its marinade, stock cube, salt, black pepper, and

tomato paste. Discard the bay leaf and cover the lid to cook for 10 minutes. Add 1 ½ tablespoon flour, mix, and cook until the soup thickens. Stir in the egg and cook for 5 minutes. Garnish with thyme. Serve warm.

Portuguese Bean Soup

Preparation time: 15 minutes
Cook time: 2 hours 40 minutes
Nutrition facts (per serving): 68 cal (13g fat, 13.3g protein, 3g fiber)

This Portuguese bean soup is an entrée that you must serve at any festive celebration. This recipe will add a lot of appeal and color to your dinner table.

Ingredients (6 servings)
1 ham hock
1 (10 ounces) linguica sausage, sliced
1 onion, minced
2 quarts water
4 potatoes, peeled and cubed
2 celery rib, chopped
2 carrots, chopped
1 (15 ounces) can stewed tomatoes
1 (8 ounces) can tomato sauce
1 garlic clove, minced
½ head cabbage, sliced
1 (15 ounces) can kidney beans

Preparation
Add water, onion, linguica, and ham hock to a Dutch oven and place it over high heat. Cook the mixture to a boil and then reduce the heat. Cover and cook on a simmer for 1 hour. Remove the meat from the pot and chop it before returning to the pot. Add the garlic, tomato sauce, tomatoes, carrots, celery, and potatoes, then cover and cook for 1 ½ hour on a simmer. Add the kidney beans and cabbage and then cook for 10 minutes. Serve warm.

Portuguese Chicken Soup

Preparation time: 5 minutes
Cook time: 35 minutes
Nutrition facts (per serving): 159 cal (7.1g fat, 17g protein, 1.8g fiber)

A perfect mix of chicken and noodles is all that you need to expand your Portuguese menu. Simple and easy to make, this recipe is a winner!

Ingredients (6 servings)
1 bone-in chicken breast
1 onion, cut into wedges
4 sprigs fresh parsley
½ teaspoon lemon zest
1 sprig of fresh mint
6 cups chicken stock
⅓ cup thin egg noodles
2 tablespoons fresh mint leaves, chopped
Salt to taste
¼ teaspoon white pepper

Preparation
Add the mint sprig, lemon zest, parsley, onion, chicken bread, and stock to a saucepan. Cook for 35 minutes and then remove the chicken from the pot. Slice the chicken into pieces. Strain the remaining broth and add to a saucepan. Add the chopped mint, pasta, white pepper, and salt. Cook until the pasta is soft. Stir in the chicken slices and lemon juice. Garnish with lemon slices and mint leaf. Serve warm.

Tomato Soup with Eggs (*Sopa de Tomate*)

Preparation time: 15 minutes
Cook time: 1 hour 32 minutes
Nutrition facts (per serving): 358 cal (14g fat, 9g protein, 4g fiber)

You can give this tomato soup a try because of its delicious combination of tomatoes with poached eggs.

Ingredients (6 servings)
4 bacon slices, cut into pieces
¼ lb. cured Portuguese chorizo sausage, sliced
6 garlic cloves, minced
2 (28-ounces) cans whole peeled tomatoes, crushed
Salt and black pepper, to taste
6 eggs
6 Portuguese Pão slices, lightly toasted

Preparation
Sauté the bacon in a 6 qt. saucepan for 10 minutes and then transfer to a plate. Add the sausage to the same pan and sauté for 5 minutes. Transfer the sausage to a plate. Add the onions to the same pan and sauté for 10 minutes. Add the garlic and sauté for 2 minutes. Add 2 cups water, black pepper, salt, and tomatoes and then cook on medium-low heat for 1 hour. Puree the soup in a blender and then return to the pan. Crack one egg into the soup at a time and cook for 5 minutes. Serve warm with bread.

Main Dishes

Codfish with Cream

Preparation time: 10 minutes
Cook time: 65 minutes
Nutrition facts (per serving): 226 cal (27g fat, 48g protein, 2g fiber)

Try this Portuguese codfish with cream with your favorite fresh herbs on top. Adding a dollop of cream or cheese will make it even richer in taste.

Ingredients (4 servings)
12 ounces dried salted codfish
Vegetable oil for frying
4 potatoes, peeled and cut into cubes
½ cup olive oil
1 large onion, sliced
3 garlic cloves, minced
1 tablespoon butter
1 tablespoon all-purpose flour
1 cup hot milk
1 pinch ground nutmeg
1⅓ cups heavy cream
Salt and black pepper to taste
⅔ cup heavy cream
1-ounce Parmesan cheese, grated

Preparation
Soak the cod in the salted cold water in a bowl for 24 hours and then drain the cod. At 350 degrees F, preheat your oven. Place the cod in a suitable saucepan, pour in enough water to cover, and cook for 10 minutes. Remove the cod from the water and then discard the skin and bones from the fish. Cut the cod into chunks. Add ½ inch oil to a large skillet over medium-high heat and fry the potatoes for almost 5 minutes, then transfer to a plate lined with a paper towel. Sauté the garlic and onion with oil in a Dutch oven for

5 minutes. Toss in the cod chunks and cook for 3 minutes. Add the potatoes and cook for 2 minutes.

Reduce the heat to low. Add the melted butter to a pan and stir in flour. Mix well on low heat, stir in the hot milk, mix thoroughly, and cook until the mixture thickens. Add nutmeg, cream, black pepper, and salt, then mix well. Spread the cod and potatoes mixture in a casserole dish and pour the cream mixture on top. Drizzle cheese on top. Bake the casserole for 40 minutes in the preheated oven. Slice and serve.

Portuguese Potato Cod Casserole (*Bacalau*)

Preparation time: 10 minutes
Cook time: 40 minutes
Nutrition facts (per serving): 701 cal (31g fat, 77g protein, 6g fiber)

Make this Portuguese Bacalau in no time and enjoy it with some garnish on top. It has layers of cod, potatoes, and eggs, which make it super-rich.

Ingredients (6 servings)
2 pounds dried salted codfish
4 Yukon Gold potatoes
3 tablespoons butter
2 yellow onions, sliced
2 garlic cloves, chopped
½ cup fresh parsley, chopped
¾ cup olive oil
1 ½ teaspoon red pepper flakes
Black pepper to taste
4 hard-cooked eggs, chopped
10 pitted green olives
10 pitted black olives

Preparation
Soak the cod in salted water for 24 hours, and then remove it from the water. Transfer the cod to a pan and pour in enough water to cover. Cook the cod for 5 minutes, then transfer to a plate. Add the potatoes and cook for 20 minutes until they are soft. Meanwhile, remove the cod skin and bones. Flake the cod in a bowl using a bowl. Mix black pepper, red pepper flakes, 1 tablespoon parsley, 1 garlic clove, and olive oil in a small bowl.

Drain the potatoes and slice them. Sauté the onions with butter in a skillet until caramelized. Stir in the garlic and sauté for almost 1 minute. Place half of the onion slices in a greased 8x11 casserole dish; top them with half of the cod, and half of the onion's mixture. Then repeat the layers with the remaining half of the potato slices, cod, and onion. Bake the casserole for 15 minutes. Garnish with the hard-cooked eggs, black and green olives, and parsley. Serve.

Portuguese Pork Alentejana

Preparation time: 15 minutes
Cook time: 15 minutes
Nutrition facts (per serving): 315 cal (12g fat, 28 protein, 2g fiber)

The pork Alentejana is quite famous in the region; in fact, and it's a favorite because of its nutritional content.

Ingredients (6 servings)
1 ½ cups dry white wine
1 teaspoon paprika
2 ½ teaspoons salt
¼ teaspoon black pepper
2 garlic cloves, peeled and halved
1 bay leaf
2 pounds pork loin, cut into cubes
3 teaspoons olive oil
2 onions, peeled and sliced
2 teaspoons garlic, chopped
2 tomatoes, peeled and chopped
¼ teaspoon crushed red pepper flakes
24 small clams in the shell, scrubbed
¼ cup fresh parsley, chopped

Preparation
Add the black pepper, salt, paprika, and wine to a bowl, and then mix well. Stir in the meat, bay leaf, and garlic cloves, and then mix well. Cover and marinate the meat for 6 hours. Transfer the prepared pork to a plate and discard the bay leaf and garlic. Sauté pork cubes with 1 teaspoon oil in a large skillet and sauté until brown. Transfer to a bowl. Pour the remaining marinade into the skillet and cook to a boil, and then cook on a simmer until it is reduced to half. Pour the marinade over the pork.

Sauté the onion with 2 teaspoons oil in a 6-quart pan for 5 minutes. Stir in the red pepper, tomatoes, and garlic, then sauté for 5 minutes. Add the tomato sauce and clams, and then cover the pan. Cook until the clams open. Stir in the juices and pork, and then cook for 5 minutes on a simmer. Garnish with parsley. Enjoy.

Portuguese Steamed Clams

Preparation time: 10 minutes
Cook time: 15 minutes
Nutrition facts (per serving): 697 cal (53g fat, 30g protein, 3g fiber)

The steamed clams are everything I was looking for. Those enjoy clams can try this simple and easy to cook recipe.

Ingredients (10 servings)
5 pounds clams in the shell, scrubbed
1 ½ pounds chorizo, sliced
1 large onion, cut into wedges
1 (14.5 ounces) can tomatoes, diced
2 cups white wine
¼ cup olive oil

Preparation
Add the clams to a stockpot and add wine, tomatoes, onion, and sausage. Cover and cook until the clams open up. Finally, drizzle olive oil on top. Serve.

Shrimp Mozambique

Preparation time: 15 minutes
Cook time: 10 minutes
Nutrition facts (per serving): 227 cal (13g fat, 20g protein, 2g fiber)

You won't know until you try it! That's what people told me about Shrimp Mozambique, and it indeed tasted more unique and flavorsome than shrimp stews I've tried.

Ingredients (4 servings)
4 tablespoons butter
¼ cup onion, chopped
½ cup of water
1 lemon, juiced
8 garlic cloves, chopped
2 (1 ½ ounce) packages Sazon seasoning
Salt and black pepper to taste
½ (12 ounces) bottle beer
2 teaspoons hot sauce
1-pound medium shrimp, peeled and deveined

Preparation
Sauté the onion with butter in a suitable saucepan over medium heat for 5 minutes. Stir in black pepper, salt, Sazon, garlic, lemon juice, and water, then cook for 2 minutes. Stir in the beer and hot sauce, and then cook the mixture to a boil. Stir in the shrimp and cook for almost 3 minutes. Serve warm.

Portuguese Sausage Kale Soup (*Caldo Verde*)

Preparation time: 15 minutes
Cook time: 65 minutes
Nutrition facts (per serving): 565 cal (26g fat, 25g protein, 4g fiber)

If you haven't tried the classic Caldo Verde before, then here comes an authentic, simple, and easy to cook recipe that you can recreate easily.

Ingredients (6 servings)
12 ounces linguica sausage, sliced
1 tablespoon olive oil
1 onion, diced
1 pinch salt
3 pounds russet potatoes, peeled and sliced
2 teaspoons salt
2 quarts chicken broth
2 pounds kale, chopped
1 pinch cayenne pepper

Preparation
Sauté the sausage with oil in a pot over medium-high heat for 5 minutes until brown. Transfer the sausage to a plate, add the onion and a pinch of salt to the same pot and cook for 5 minutes. Stir in the potatoes, 2 teaspoons salt, and chicken broth. Cook on a simmer for 10 minutes. Once soft, lightly mash the potatoes with a fork. Stir in the kale and sausage and cook on a simmer for 45 minutes.

Portuguese Beef Stew

Preparation time: 15 minutes
Cook time: 80 minutes
Nutrition facts (per serving): 398 cal (12g fat, 27g protein, 4g fiber)

This beef stew is loved by all, young and adult. It's simple and quick to make. This delight is great to serve at dinner tables.

Ingredients (4 servings)
2 tablespoons olive oil
1-pound stew meat, cut into cubes
1 tablespoon all-purpose flour
8 garlic cloves, minced
2 bay leaves
1 pinch black pepper
1 pinch salt
1 onion, chopped
1 green bell pepper, chopped
1 carrot, chopped
1 pinch paprika
½ fresh tomato, chopped
1 cup white wine
1 cup of water
2 sprigs fresh parsley
3 red potatoes, peeled and cubed
1 sweet potato, peeled and cubed
1 (14.5 ounces) can green beans, drained

Preparation
Dust the beef with flour. Add the oil, dusted beef, black pepper, bay leaves, and garlic to a saucepan. Sauté until the beef is brown. Stir in the paprika, carrot, green pepper, and onion, then sauté for 5 minutes. Add the parsley,

water, wine, and tomatoes, cover, and cook for 30 minutes on a simmer. Add the red potatoes, green beans, and sweet potatoes, cook for 45 minutes. Serve warm.

Seafood Bread Stew (*Açorda de Marisco*)

Preparation time: 5 minutes
Cook time: 15 minutes
Nutrition facts (per serving): 433 cal (6.8g fat, 73g protein, 3g fiber)

Try the bread stew at the dinner as the bread is infused with amazing flavors of seafood broth. Serve warm with your favorite sauces.

Ingredients (6 servings)
21 ounces (600 g) clams
21 ounces (600 g) cockles
22 ounces shrimp
21 ounces (600 g) crusty bread in pieces
4 cloves garlic
1 tablespoon oil
1 bunch coriander, chopped
4 eggs
Salt, to taste
Black pepper, to taste
Chili

Preparation
Boil the shrimp in salted water for almost 2 minutes, then transfer to a bowl. Add the clams and cockles to the boiling water and cook to a boil. Spread the bread pieces in a bowl and pour the clams water over it to soak. Sauté the garlic with olive oil in a suitable saucepan until brown. Stir in coriander, and squeeze the bread. Add the prawns, eggs, clams, cockle, chili, black pepper, salt, and serve.

Portuguese Shrimps

Preparation time: 5 minutes
Cook time: 25 minutes
Nutrition facts (per serving): 147 cal (3g fat, 20g protein, 3g fiber)

Simple and easy to make, this recipe is a must to try on this menu. This dish is a delight for the dinner table.

Ingredients (6 servings)
1 tablespoon olive oil
1 onion, chopped
3 garlic cloves, minced
1 (12 ounces) can of ale (or similar beer)
5 sprigs parsley, stemmed and chopped
2 teaspoons tomato paste
2 teaspoons Portuguese hot pepper sauce
1 cube chicken bouillon
1 teaspoon ground paprika
2 pounds large shrimp, deveined
1 teaspoon salt

Preparation
Sauté the onion and garlic with olive oil in a skillet for 5 minutes. Stir in the paprika, half of the ale, chicken bouillon, hot pepper sauce, tomato paste, and parsley, and then cook for 5 minutes. Stir in the shrimp, salt, and remaining ale. Cook for 15-20 minutes until the shrimp change their color. Serve warm.

Portuguese Rice (*Arroz de Braga*)

Preparation time: 5 minutes
Cook time: 50 minutes
Nutrition facts (per serving): 539 cal (20g fat, 26g protein, 4g fiber)

Portuguese Rice is one of the traditional Portuguese entrées made from rice, sausage, and ham, etc.

Ingredients (6 servings)
2 tablespoons vegetable oil
1 onion, chopped
½ pound chicken thighs, diced
½ pound chicken drumsticks, boneless and diced
2 teaspoons salt
7 ounces ham, cubed and cooked
2 pork sausages, smoked, sliced
2 links pork sausage, sliced
3 cups rice, rinsed and drained
4 tomatoes, chopped
1 red bell pepper, sliced
2 spring onions, chopped
1 teaspoon parsley, chopped
6 cups of water
2 cubes chicken bouillon
3 cabbage leaves, sliced
1 tablespoon olive oil

Preparation
Sauté the onion with drumsticks and chicken thighs in a cooking pot for 10 minutes. Stir in the sausages and ham, and then cook for 10 minutes. Add the parsley, salt, spring onion, red bell pepper, tomatoes, water, chicken bouillon, and rice. Partially cover the pot and cook on a simmer for 15

minutes. Add the sliced cabbage and cook for another 15 minutes. Garnish with olive oil and serve warm.

Green Cabbage (*Caldo Verde*)

Preparation time: 15 minutes
Cook time: 26 minutes
Nutrition facts (per serving): 456 cal (27g fat, 11g protein, 4g fiber)

Do you want to enjoy a cabbage stew with a Portuguese twist? Then try this Portuguese cabbage Caldo Verde recipe. You can serve it with your favorite bread.

Ingredients (6 servings)
3 tablespoons olive oil
1 onion, chopped
3 garlic cloves, crushed
6 potatoes, peeled and sliced
1-pound cabbage, sliced
2 quarts water
8 ounces Portuguese chorizo sausage, sliced
1 teaspoon smoked paprika
2 teaspoons salt
Black pepper to taste
Olive oil

Preparation
Sauté the garlic and onion with 3 tablespoons oil in a Dutch oven for 3 minutes. Stir in half of the cabbage and sliced potatoes, and then sauté for 3 minutes. Add water and cook the mixture to a boil. Reduce the heat, cover, and cook for 15 minutes on a simmer. Puree the soup until smooth. Stir in the black pepper, salt, paprika, remaining cabbage, and sausage, then cover and cook on a simmer for 5 minutes. Serve warm with a drizzle of olive oil on top.

Portuguese Beef Shish Kabobs (*Espetadas*)

Preparation time: 15 minutes
Cook time: 8 minutes
Nutrition facts (per serving): 190 cal (7.8g fat, 23.8g protein, 3g fiber)

The classic Portuguese beef kabobs are here to complete your Portuguese menu. This meal can be served on all special occasions and festive celebrations, especially on a BBQ night.

Ingredients (6 servings)
¾ cup red wine
8 garlic cloves
6 bay leaves, crumbled
2 tablespoons salt
Black pepper to taste
3 pounds beef sirloin steak, cubed

Preparation
Mix the black pepper, salt, bay leaves, and red wine in a large suitable bowl. Toss in the sirloin cubes and cover to refrigerate for 8 hours. Preheat and prepare a grill over medium-high heat. Thread the beef on the skewers and grill the beef for 4 minutes per side. Serve warm.

Portuguese Rice and Beans (*JAG*)

Preparation time: 15 minutes
Cook time: 40 minutes
Nutrition facts (per serving): 562 cal (34g fat, 19g protein, 3.2g fiber)

The Portuguese rice and bean recipe is here to complete your Portuguese menu. This meal can be served on all special occasions and memorable celebrations.

Ingredients (4 servings)

½ cup butter
1 large onion, chopped
1 green bell pepper, chopped
1 red bell pepper, chopped
1-pound linguica sausage, cut into cubes
1 teaspoon black pepper
1 teaspoon dried basil
½ teaspoon dried oregano
1 (15.5 ounces) can shelled beans
2½ cups water
2 cups white rice

Preparation

Sauté the onion, bell peppers, oregano, basil, black pepper, and sauté in a cooking pot for 15 minutes. Add the beans and cook for 5 minutes. Stir in the rice and water, then cover and cook for 25 minutes on low heat until rice is soft. Serve warm.

Portuguese Beef Roast Sopas

Preparation time: 15 minutes
Cook time: 4 hours 30 minutes
Nutrition facts (per serving): 464 cal (32g fat, 34g protein, 5g fiber)

It's about time to try some classic beef roast sopas on the menu and make it more diverse and flavorsome. Serve warm with your favorite herbs on top.

Ingredients (6 servings)
1 (3 pounds) beef pot roast
1 onion, diced
1 cup fresh mint leaves
2 garlic cloves, minced
2 teaspoons ground cinnamon
2 teaspoons ground allspice
2 bay leaves
Salt and black pepper to taste
Water to cover
1 head cabbage, quartered

Preparation
Add the pot roast, bay leaves, allspice, cinnamon, garlic, mint, onion, black pepper, and salt to a cooking pot and pour enough water over the pot roast to cover it. Cook the meat for 4 hours on a simmer. Add the cabbage wedges and cook for 30 minutes on a simmer. Serve warm.

Portuguese Style Beef Steaks

Preparation time: 15 minutes
Cook time: 6 minutes
Nutrition facts (per serving): 467 cal (39g fat, 21g protein, 3g fiber)

This recipe is always an easy way to add extra proteins and nutrients to your menu, and here some that you can make in just a few minutes.

Ingredients (6 servings)
¾ cup red wine
¼ cup of water
10 garlic cloves, chopped
1 tablespoon chili paste
½ teaspoon white pepper
½ teaspoon salt
6 (4 ounces) beef tenderloin steaks
⅓ cup vegetable oil

Preparation
Mix the beef with salt, white pepper, chili paste, water, and red wine in a medium bowl. Add beef to a greased skillet for 2 minutes per side. Once seared, add the marinade to the beef and cook for 2 minutes on a boil. Serve warm.

Portuguese Chicken

Preparation time: 15 minutes
Cook time: 45 minutes
Nutrition facts (per serving): 492 cal (35g fat, 40g protein, 6g fiber)

If you haven't tried the Portuguese chicken, then here comes an authentic, simple, and easy to cook recipe that you can dazzle at home in minimum time.

Ingredients (4 servings)
¼ cup lemon juice
4 tablespoons olive oil
4 garlic cloves, peeled
1 tablespoon paprika
1 teaspoon dried oregano
1 teaspoon of sea salt
1 teaspoon chili powder
1 teaspoon red pepper flakes
1 bay leaf
½ teaspoon black pepper
4 chicken leg quarters
1 pinch sea salt

Preparation
Blend the black pepper, bay leaf, red pepper flakes, chili powder, 1 teaspoon salt, oregano, paprika, garlic, lemon juice, and oil in a blender for 1 minute. Score the chicken legs with a knife and place them in a bowl. Pour the marinade over the chicken. Rub the chicken with the paste and refrigerate for 8 hours. Spread the chicken in a baking dish and cover them with aluminum foil. Bake the chicken for almost 25 minutes at 350 degrees F. Turn the chicken, baste with the marinade, cover again, and bake again for 20 minutes. Serve warm.

Wine Garlic Pork (*Vina Dosh*)

Preparation time: 15 minutes
Cook time: 35 minutes
Nutrition facts (per serving): 291 cal (20g fat, 18g protein, 2g fiber)

Quite famous for its unique taste and aroma, this dish is perfect to bring home those exotic flavors!

Ingredients (6 servings)
1½ cups red wine vinegar
¾ cup red wine
7 garlic cloves, crushed
½ teaspoon dried thyme
3 bay leaves
8 whole cloves
2 tablespoons black pepper, ground
2 teaspoons salt
1 (3 pounds) boneless pork shoulder, cubed
2 tablespoons vegetable oil

Preparation
Mix the thyme, salt, black pepper, cloves, bay leaves, garlic, red wine, and red wine vinegar in a bowl. Add this prepared mixture to a Ziploc bag along with pork, seal the bag, and shake the bag to cover the pork. Marinate the seasoned pork for 2 days in the refrigerator and shake the bag after every 12 hours. At 350 degrees F, preheat your oven. Transfer the pork and ½ cup marinade to a baking dish. Bake the pork for 20 minutes in the oven, and then remove the meat from the marinade. Sauté the pork with oil in a skillet over medium heat for 15 minutes until brown. Serve warm.

Portuguese Patty Melts

Preparation time: 15 minutes
Cook time: 22 minutes
Nutrition facts (per serving): 672 cal (31g fat, 48g protein, 4g fiber)

These patty melts are a staple for every fancy dinner. Plus, and with the help of this recipe, you can cook them in no time.

Ingredients (4 servings)
1 ½ pounds ground beef
2 garlic cloves, minced
1 tablespoon water
Black pepper to taste
¼ cup olive oil
2 large sweet onions, sliced
½ teaspoon ground cumin
1 (4 ounces) link linguica sausage, sliced into quarters
4 American cheese, slices
8 deli rye bread slices
2 tablespoons butter, softened
4 teaspoons Dijon mustard

Preparation
Mix the black pepper, water, garlic, and ground beef in a bowl, then make 4 patties. Place the patties in a sheet, cover, and refrigerate. Sauté the onion and cumin with oil in medium-high heat for 7 minutes until brown, then transfer to a bowl. Stir in the sausage and cook for 2 minutes per side. Transfer the sausages to a plate. Sear the patties in the same skillet for 5 minutes per side. Then place a cheese slice on top and cook the patties for 2 minutes and transfer to a plate. Grease a bread slice with butter and sear the bread until brown and crispy. Place a patty on top of one bread slice. Add

the onion and mustard on top and place another bread slice on top. Toast the sandwiches for 2 minutes per side in a skillet.

Portuguese Braised Chicken

Preparation time: 15 minutes
Cook time: 65 minutes
Nutrition facts (per serving): 540 cal (39g fat, 37g protein, 8g fiber)

The delicious braised chicken always tastes great when you cook the chicken with lots of herbs and spices using this recipe.

Ingredients (5 servings)
1 tablespoon olive oil
¼ pound linguica sausage, sliced
½ onion, sliced
½ green bell pepper, chopped
2 pounds of chicken parts
¾ teaspoon fresh oregano. chopped
⅛ teaspoon fresh basil, chopped
½ teaspoon salt
¼ teaspoon black pepper
½ cup dry white wine
½ cup 1 teaspoon chicken broth
1 bay leaves
⅛ teaspoon red pepper flakes
½ orange, cut into wedges

Preparation
Sauté the bell pepper, onion, and sausage with oil in a Dutch oven for 10 minutes and transfer to a plate. Rub the chicken with black pepper, salt, basil, and oregano and sear the chicken for 10 minutes in the same pot over medium-high heat. Add the vegetable mixture, sausage, red pepper flakes, bay leaves, broth, and wine, and then cook the mixture to a boil. Reduce the heat, cover, and cook for 45 minutes on a simmer. Serve warm.

Portuguese Stuffing Balls

Preparation time: 15 minutes
Cook time: 35 minutes
Nutrition facts (per serving): 558 cal (30g fat, 9.8g protein, 3g fiber)

Are you in a mood to have stuffing balls on the menu? Well, you can try this simple and easy to make recipe at home.

Ingredients (6 servings)
1 ½ loaf white bread, torn into pieces
¼ cup water
½ egg, beaten
¾ cup lard
1 sweet onion, chopped
¼ cup parsley, chopped
2 tablespoons 2 teaspoons cider vinegar
1 teaspoon red pepper flakes
¼ teaspoon salt
¼ teaspoon black pepper
Cooking spray

Preparation
Place the bread pieces in a large suitable bowl, pour water and egg over the bread, and mix well. Sauté the onion and parsley with lard in a large skillet for 10 minutes. Reduce its heat to low and add black pepper, salt, red pepper flakes, and vinegar. Cook for 5 minutes. Add this prepared mixture over bread and mix well. At 325 degrees F, preheat your oven. Grease 2 baking sheets with cooking spray. Make 3-inch balls out of this prepared mixture and place them on the baking sheets. Bake the stuffing balls for 20 minutes in the oven and serve warm.

Portuguese Rabbit

Preparation time: 10 minutes
Cook time: 60 minutes
Nutrition facts (per serving): 570 cal (30g fat, 49g protein, 3g fiber)

Have you tried the Portuguese rabbit meal? Well, now you can enjoy this unique and flavorsome combination by cooking this recipe at home.

Ingredients (4 servings)
1 (2 pounds) rabbit, cut into pieces
Salt and black pepper to taste
3 tablespoons mustard
3 tablespoons vegetable oil
1 cup white wine
4 small onions
2 slices bacon, cut into pieces
1 orange

Preparation
At 350 degrees F, preheat the oven. Rub the rabbit with black pepper, salt, and mustard and place the rabbit in the Dutch oven. Add the white wine, onions, bacon pieces, and oil around the rabbit, then cover and bake for 30 minutes in the oven. Remove the lid, add the orange juice, bake for 30 minutes, and then serve warm.

Chorizo Potato Stew

Preparation time: 15 minutes
Cook time: 40 minutes
Nutrition facts (per serving): 378 cal (22g fat, 14g protein, 3.6g fiber)

Portuguese chicken potato stew is always served as a complete meal. In particular, this one is great to have on a nutritious diet.

Ingredients (6 servings)
4 cups of water
1 (16 ounces) package chorizo sausage, diced
2 potatoes, diced
½ head cabbage, chopped
3 carrots, diced
1 small onion, chopped
1 stalk celery, diced
1 (15 ounces) can mixed vegetables, drained
2 tablespoons parsley, chopped
½ teaspoon garlic powder
½ teaspoon celery salt
½ teaspoon ground red pepper
2 tablespoons cornstarch
2 tablespoons water

Preparation
Add the chorizo, water, cabbage, potatoes, canned vegetables, onion, carrots, celery, parsley, celery salt, garlic powder, and red pepper to a large pot. Cook the mixture on a simmer for 40 minutes. Mix the cornstarch with water in a bowl and pour into the pot and cook until the mixture thickens. Serve warm.

Pan-Fried Hake

Preparation time: 15 minutes
Cook time: 25 minutes
Nutrition facts (per serving): 338 cal (20g fat, 13g protein, 3g fiber)

Now you can quickly make a flavorsome pan-fried hake with tomato sauce and serve as a fancy meal for yourself and your guest.

Ingredients (4 servings)
Sauce
2 ripe tomatoes
3 tablespoons olive oil
2 bay leaves
3 whole allspice berries, chopped
4 garlic cloves, minced
1 green bell pepper, sliced
1 onion, sliced
¼ cup dry white wine
½ cup black olives, pitted
Salt and black pepper, to taste

Fish
¼ cup olive oil
2-pounds hake fillets, cut into four portions
Black pepper, to taste
2 cups cornmeal

Preparation
Add water to fill half of a saucepan and boil it over high heat. Carve an X on top of each tomato and place them in the boiling water and cook for 30 seconds. Transfer the tomatoes to an ice bath and then peel their skin. Slice them in half, remove the seeds, and then slice them into strips.

Sauté the bay leaves with 3 tablespoons oil in a skillet over medium-high heat for 3 minutes. Stir in the onion and bell pepper, then sauté for 5 minutes. Add the olives, white wine, and tomatoes and cook for 5 minutes. Add the black pepper and salt, remove it from the heat. Coat the hake fillets with black pepper and cornmeal and then sear them in a skillet with ¼ cup olive oil for 4 minutes per side. Serve the fish with prepared sauce. Enjoy.

Portuguese Grilled Lobsters

Preparation time: 10 minutes
Cook time: 23 minutes
Nutrition facts (per serving): 321 cal (20g fat, 24g protein, g fiber)

Grilled lobsters are always a delight on a menu. Now you can cook these lobsters easily at home by using the following simple ingredients.

Ingredients (4 servings)
4 (1 ½-pound) live lobsters
12 tablespoons unsalted butter
¼ cup olive oil
⅓-pound linguica, chopped
6 garlic cloves, chopped
1 ¾ cups panko
¼ cup parsley, chopped
3 tablespoons chives, minced
Juice of 1 lemon
Salt and black pepper, to taste

Preparation
Prepare and preheat a grill over medium heat. Sauté the sausage with butter and olive oil in a skillet for 2 minutes. Stir in the garlic and sauté for almost 1 minute. Transfer ½ of the fat from the skillet to a cup. Stir in the panko and sauté for 5 minutes. Stir in the black pepper, salt, lemon juice, chives, and parsley. Brush the lobster tail with the ½ of the reserved fat and pack the tail with a breadcrumb mixture. Place the lobster tail in aluminum and transfer to the grill. Next, cover and cook for 15 minutes. Garnish with lemon wedges and parsley. Serve warm.

Portuguese Seafood Cataplana

Preparation time: 10 minutes
Cook time: 7 minutes
Nutrition facts (per serving): 378 cal (11g fat, 25g protein, 3g fiber)

If you haven't tried the seafood cataplana before, then here comes an authentic, simple, and easy to cook recipe that you can recreate easily at home today!

Ingredients (4 servings)
1 tablespoon olive oil
1-ounce linguica sausage
1 ½ tablespoon shallot, sliced
1 ½ tablespoon garlic, chopped
1-pound fresh manila clams
1 ½ ounces shrimp, peeled and deveined
¼ cup vine ripe tomatoes crushed
2 tablespoons white wine
Smoked paprika, to taste
Salt and black pepper, to taste
1 tablespoon parsley, chopped
1 lemon, cut into wedges, for serving

Preparation
Add 1 teaspoon oil and sausage in a cataplana pan and sauté until brown. Stir in the garlic and shallots and then sauté for 2 minutes. Add the paprika, wine, tomatoes, shrimp, clams, black pepper, and salt. Cover and cook on medium-low heat for almost 5 minutes. Garnish with lemon juice, parsley, and oil. Serve warm.

One-Pot Chicken and Potatoes

Preparation time: 10 minutes
Cook time: 18 minutes
Nutrition facts (per serving): 391 cal (7g fat, 27g protein, 2g fiber)

Try cooking the delicious one-pot chicken with some unique combination of spices and potatoes at home to enjoy the best of the Portuguese flavors now.

Ingredients (8 servings)
8 skinless chicken thighs, bone-in
Salt and black pepper, to taste
1 cup all-purpose flour
2 tablespoons sweet paprika
¼ cup olive oil
4 ounces chorizo, chopped
1 ½ pounds potatoes, quartered
2 tablespoons chopped fresh thyme
3 garlic cloves, sliced
2 small stalks celery, sliced
1 large bay leaf
1 Fresno chili pepper, sliced
1 onion, chopped
⅓ cup dry sherry
1 cup chicken stock
1 teaspoon lemon zest, grated
1 teaspoon orange zest, grated
1 (14-ounce) can chunky crushed tomatoes
1 handful parsley, chopped
4 Portuguese rolls

Preparation

Mix the flour, black pepper, paprika, and salt in a bowl. Dredge the chicken through the flour and coat well. Add 3 tablespoons of oil to a Dutch oven over medium-high heat and sear the chicken until golden brown from all the sides. Transfer the seared chicken to a plate. Add the remaining 1 tablespoon oil and add chorizo, then sauté until brown.

Transfer to the chicken. Add the onions, chili peppers, bay leaf, celery, garlic, thyme, and potatoes to the same pot and sauté for 8 minutes. Stir in the sherry, tomatoes, orange and lemon zest, and stock. Mix and deglaze the pot, then return the chorizo and chicken to the pot and cook for 10 minutes. Garnish with parsley and Portuguese rolls. Serve warm.

Fisherman's Shrimp and Chorizo

Preparation time: 10 minutes
Cook time: 20 minutes
Nutrition facts (per serving): 492 cal (13g fat, 39g protein, 0.5g fiber)

This fisherman's shrimp and chorizo recipe is something special to try for dinner. Cook in just 20 minutes and serve with toasted bread.

Ingredients (6 servings)
1 tablespoon olive oil
8 ounces chorizo, chopped
1 potato, peeled and chopped
1 onion, chopped
1 carrot, peeled and chopped
3 garlic cloves, chopped
1 Fresno chili pepper, sliced
2 tablespoons fresh thyme, chopped
1 bay leaf
1 small bunch kale, chopped
1 dash nutmeg, grated
1 (15-ounce) can chickpeas, drained
1 (15-ounce) can diced tomatoes
3 cups chicken stock
Salt and black pepper, to taste
1 ½ pounds medium shrimp, deveined
Juice of 1 lemon
Portuguese rolls, for serving

Preparation
Sauté the chorizo with 1 tablespoon oil in a Dutch oven for 2 minutes. Stir in the bay leaf, thyme, the chile pepper, garlic, carrot, onion, and potato, then sauté for 6 minutes. Add the kale, nutmeg, chickpeas, stock, tomatoes,

black pepper, and salt, then cook to a boil, then reduce the heat to low. Add the shrimp and lemon juice and cook for almost 4 minutes. Serve warm with olive oil on top and Portuguese rolls. Enjoy.

Portuguese Mussels

Preparation time: 10 minutes
Cook time: 16 minutes
Nutrition facts (per serving): 457 cal (19g fat, 23g protein, 5g fiber)

Portuguese mussels are one delicious way to complete your Portuguese menu; here's a recipe that you can try to have a complete meal.

Ingredients (6 servings)
3 tablespoons butter
1 teaspoon garlic, minced
½ French loaf bread
3 pounds mussels
1 cup ground Portuguese chorizo
½ large onion, sliced
½ green pepper, sliced
½ red pepper, sliced
½ cup Riesling wine

Preparation
At 350 degrees F, preheat your oven. Mix the garlic with 1 tablespoon butter. Cut the French bread in half and brush its crumb with the butter mixture. Place the bread in a baking sheet and bake for 10 minutes in the oven. Add 2 tablespoons of butter and chorizo to a saucepan, then sauté for almost 1 minute. Stir in the red peppers, green peppers, and onion, then sauté for almost 1 minute. Add ½ cup of water and wine. Cook until warm, then add mussels, and cover to cook for almost 4 minutes. Serve warm with the toasted bread.

Portuguese Prego Rolls

Preparation time: 10 minutes
Cook time: 20 minutes
Nutrition facts (per serving): 391 cal (17g fat, 50g protein, 14g fiber)

Let's make some Prego rolls with these simple ingredients. Use some peri-peri sauce to season the meat and serve with buns and bread.

Ingredients (4 servings)
Marinade
3 tablespoons Peri-Peri sauce
½ cup tomato puree
2 tablespoons lemon juice
2 garlic cloves
1 bay leaf
2 tablespoons olive oil
1 teaspoon sugar (optional)
1-2 teaspoons salt

Prego rolls
4 sirloin steaks sliced in half
4 bread rolls
Sliced tomato
Sliced onion
Chili butter
1-2 fresh chilies, chopped
½ cup butter

Preparation
Blend all the prego marinade ingredients in a blender until smooth. Spread the steaks in a tray, rub the marinade over them, and cover to refrigerate for 30 minutes. Grill the steak in a greased griddle pan for 5-10 minutes per side

until brown. Transfer the steaks to a plate. Mix the chilies with butter in a bowl. Cut the bread rolls in half and layer them with chili butter. Add the cooked steak to the roll with the onion and tomato slices. Serve.

Piri-Piri Chicken with Potatoes

Preparation time: 10 minutes
Cook time: 30 minutes
Nutrition facts (per serving): 359 cal (5 g fat, 33g protein, 1g fiber)

Count on this Piri-Piri chicken with potatoes to make your dinner extra special and surprise your loved one with the ultimate flavors.

Ingredients (8 servings)
1 pound Yukon Gold potatoes, cubed
7 tablespoons olive oil
Salt and black pepper, to taste
8 chicken thighs and drumsticks
3 Fresno chili peppers, chopped
2 garlic cloves, chopped
Grated zest and juice of 1 lemon
1 tablespoon 2 teaspoons red wine vinegar
1 teaspoon paprika
½ teaspoon honey
4 cups iceberg lettuce salad mix

Preparation
Toss the potatoes with 1 tablespoon oil, black pepper, and salt on a baking sheet and roast them for 10 minutes at 475 degrees F. Sear the chicken with oil, black pepper, and salt in a skillet for almost 6 minutes per side until golden brown. Blend 1 teaspoon salt, honey, paprika, 1 tablespoon vinegar, lemon juice and lemon zest, garlic, and chilies in a blender. Stir in ¼ cup olive oil and mix well. Place the chicken on the potato's baking sheet and pour half of the sauce over the chicken and bake for 15 minutes.

Toss the lettuce with black pepper, salt, 2 teaspoons vinegar, and 1 tablespoon olive oil in a bowl. Serve the chicken with potatoes, remaining chili sauce, and lettuce mixture. Serve.

Piri-Piri Sauce

Preparation time: 10 minutes
Cook time: 4 minutes
Nutrition facts (per serving): 482 cal (13g fat, 29g protein, 6g fiber)

Since the piri-piri sauce is an important ingredient in the Portuguese cuisines, it's essential to learn the secrets behind its preparation.

Ingredients (8 servings)
Black pepper, to taste
1 tablespoon garlic, minced
1 ¼ cups olive oil
4 fresh jalapeno peppers, chopped
2 fresh poblano peppers, chopped
1 tablespoon crushed red pepper
1 teaspoon salt

Preparation
Sauté the peppers with oil, red pepper, salt, and black pepper in a saucepan for 4 minutes. Stir in the garlic, mix well, and remove it from the heat. Puree the pepper mixture until smooth in a blender. Strain the pureed sauce and store it in a glass container. Refrigerate for 7 days and then serve.

Chicken with Grapes

Preparation time: 10 minutes
Cook time: 55 minutes
Nutrition facts (per serving): 381 cal (17g fat, 27g protein, 1g fiber)

If you haven't tried the Portuguese chicken with grapes before, then here comes an authentic, simple, and easy to cook recipe that you can recreate easily at home in minimum time.

Ingredients (6 servings)
5 tablespoons butter
5 tablespoon lard
2 cups 1 tablespoon flour
Salt, to taste
4 tablespoons iced water
1 (3 pounds) chicken
½-pound bacon slices
Black pepper, to taste
1 teaspoon allspice
1 teaspoon paprika
⅓ cup dry sherry
⅓ cup sweet sherry
2 sage leaves
12-ounce seedless green grapes
1 tablespoon brown sugar
1 egg yolk

Preparation
Mix the lard, butter, ½ teaspoons salt, and 2 cups flour in a bowl. Stir in the water and mix until it makes a smooth dough. Leave the dough for ½ hour, and then roll the dough into a 10-inch sheet. Place the pie dough in a 9 inches pie pan and cut out the excess dough around the rim.

At 400 degrees F, preheat your oven. Cut the chicken into pieces and pat them dry. Sauté bacon in a skillet until brown, then chop it. Transfer it to a plate. Sear the chicken in the bacon fat and season it with paprika, allspice, black pepper, and salt, and cook for 5 minutes per side.

Transfer the chicken to the pie pan. Mix 1 tablespoon flour with the bacon fat in the same skillet. Next, stir in the sherry, mix and cook until smooth. Add chicken, ½ sage leaf, brown sugar, and grapes. Mix well and drizzle the bacon on top, then cook for 5 minutes. Brush the prepared pastry with the egg yolk and bake for 30 minutes. Serve the chicken with the pastry. Enjoy.

Garlicky Green Beans

Preparation time: 15 minutes
Cook time: 16 minutes
Nutrition facts (per serving): 412 cal (9g fat, 13g protein, 0.5g fiber)

The famous green beans are here to make your Portuguese cuisine extra special. Make it with fresh green beans and garlic for the best taste.

Ingredients (6 servings)
2 pounds green beans, washed
3 quarts boiling water,
2 large garlic cloves, peeled and minced
⅔ cup coriander leaves, chopped
5 tablespoons olive oil
1 tablespoon lemon juice
4 tablespoons cider vinegar
¼ teaspoon black pepper

Preparation
Boil the beans in salted water in a suitable saucepan for 12 minutes, then drain. Mix the coriander with garlic in a bowl. Add the beans to the bowl and toss well. Stir in 5 tablespoons olive oil, mix and refrigerate for 4 hours. Remove the beans from the refrigerator and add the black pepper, 3 tablespoons vinegar, lemon juice, salt, and olive oil, then mix well. Serve.

Pickle Meat Stew (*Macao*)

Preparation time: 10 minutes
Cook time: 38 minutes
Nutrition facts (per serving): 470 cal (12g fat, 24g protein, 6 g fiber)

This Portuguese meat stew recipe has unique pickle mixed flavors due to its rich blend of meat with veggies and pickles. Serve warm with rice or bread.

Ingredients (12 servings)
6 pounds cooked beef chunks
3 tablespoons olive oil
2 large onions, chopped
8 medium tomatoes, chopped
1 (32-ounce) jar mixed pickles, chopped
Juice from meats
3 pounds potatoes, peeled and quartered
18 eggs, hardboiled
6 tablespoons sugar
2 teaspoons powdered mustard
Vinegar from pickles
1 cup white wine
3 cups rice, cooked

Preparation
Sauté the onion with oil in a large pot until golden brown. Stir in the tomatoes and cook until their liquid is evaporated. Add the chopped meat and pickles, and then cook for 10 minutes. Stir in the water to cover the meat and potatoes and then cook for 20 minutes. Peel the boiled eggs, cut them in half, remove the yolks from the whites, and mash the whites in a bowl. Mash the yolks with mustard, sugar, and vinegar from the pickles in a bowl. Add this prepared mixture to the potatoes and cook for 5 minutes. Stir in

the white wine and cook for 3 minutes. Serve the cooked meat with mashed egg whites and rice. Serve.

Portuguese Fish Chowder

Preparation time: 10 minutes
Cook time: 35 minutes
Nutrition facts (per serving): 219 cal (12g fat, 2g protein, 1g fiber)

Best to serve at dinner, this fish chowder offers an energizing meal. It's a Portuguese version of delicious seafood soup.

Ingredients (4 servings)
2 tablespoons olive oil
2 dried bay leaves
3 garlic cloves, chopped
2 medium onions, diced
1 green bell pepper, diced
¼ teaspoon ground allspice
2 pounds Yukon potatoes, peeled and sliced
4 cups fish stock
2 cups canned whole tomatoes
6 ounces spicy chorizo, sliced
Salt and black pepper, to taste
2 pounds skinless silver hake, pin bones removed
10 sprigs fresh cilantro, leaves, and chopped
Garnish
2 tablespoons fresh Italian parsley, chopped

Preparation
Sauté the bay leaves with the olive oil in a 4-quart heavy pot for 1 minute. Stir in the garlic and sauté for almost 30 seconds. Add the allspices, bell pepper, and onions, then sauté for 8 minutes. Add the stock potatoes and enough water to cover them, and then cook for 10 minutes. Reduce the heat and add the sausage and tomatoes. Next, cook for 5 minutes. Add the black

pepper and salt, and then mix well. Place the fish fillets in the pan and cook for 10 minutes on a simmer. Garnish with parsley. Serve warm.

Seafood Rice

Preparation time: 15 minutes
Cook time: 73 minutes
Nutrition facts (per serving): 331 cal (5g fat, 19.5g protein, 5.2g fiber)

If you haven't tried the Portuguese seafood rice before, then here comes an authentic, simple, and easy to cook recipe that you can recreate quickly at home.

Ingredients (6 servings)
1 onion, chopped
2 celery sticks, chopped
2 tablespoons olive oil
6 garlic cloves, bashed
2 bay leaves
1 tablespoon paprika
½ teaspoons dried chili flakes
4 tomatoes, cored and chopped
14 ounces of canned tomatoes, chopped
1 teaspoon granulated sugar
3 ½ ounces (300 g) risotto rice
26 ounces mussels, cleaned
7 ounces peeled king prawns, defrosted
Small bunch oregano, chopped
½ bunch parsley, chopped
¼ cup butter, diced

Preparation
Sauté the celery and onion with oil in a casserole dish over medium-high heat for 10 minutes. Stir in the bay leaves and garlic then sauté for 1 second. Add the seasoning, tomatoes, chili flakes, and paprika. Cook for 1 minute, then add 6 ½ cup cold water, sugar, and tomatoes, then cover the lid. Cook the

tomatoes for 45 minutes. Add the rice and cook for 15 minutes. Add the mussels and seasoning, then cover and cook for 10 minutes. Add prawns and cook for 2 minutes. Stir in the butter, parsley, and oregano. Enjoy.

Fish Stew (*Caldeirada De Peixe*)

Preparation time: 15 minutes
Cook time: 40 minutes
Nutrition facts (per serving): 389cal (4.4g fat, 38g protein, 4.1g fiber)

This fish stew is simply irresistible due to all the colors and the aromas. Sure, it takes some time to get it ready, but its great taste is worth all the time and effort.

Ingredients (6 servings)
Olive oil
2 onions, chopped
1 red pepper, seeded and diced
1 small bunch of coriander
1 small red chili, seeded and chopped
2 garlic cloves, chopped
1 garlic clove, halved
1 ½ cups dry white wine
1 pinch saffron
1 bay leaf
10 ½ ounces potatoes, peeled and diced
14 ounces plum tomatoes tin
21ounces (600 g) skinless firm white fish, cut into large chunks
10 ½ ounces squid, cleaned and sliced
8 raw tiger prawns
20 ounces clams, cleaned
20 ounces mussels, cleaned
1 baguette, sliced

Preparation
Sauté the onion with oil in a large pan until soft. Stir in the coriander, chili, and garlic, then sauté for almost 1 minute. Add the bay leaf, saffron and

wine. Next, cook until reduced to half. Add the water, tomatoes, and potatoes, and then cook on a simmer for 25 minutes. Add the fish, clams, prawns, squid, and mussels to the stew, cover, and cook for 8 minutes. Sauté half of the garlic clove with olive oil in a skillet. Sear the bread until golden. Garnish the stew with coriander and serve warm with the toasts.

Portuguese Barbecued Pork (*Febras Assadas*)

Preparation time: 5 minutes
Cook time: 38 minutes
Nutrition facts (per serving): 809 cal (49g fat, 49.6g protein, 3.3g fiber)

This Portuguese BBQ pork recipe will make your day with a delightful taste. Serve warm with your favorite salad.

Ingredients (5 servings)
2 pork tenderloins, cut into 5 pieces
1 cup white wine
½ teaspoons smoked paprika
2 lemons, ½ juiced and rest cut into wedges
Olive oil
Mayonnaise

Preparation
Add the tenderloin pieces to a Ziploc bag. Mix the lemon juice, black pepper, salt, paprika, and wine in a bowl. Pour this prepared mixture into the bag, seal it, and shake well. Marinate the meat for 30 minutes. Add the oil to a cooking pot and sear the pork for 4 minutes per side until brown and tender. Serve warm with lemon wedges on top.

Portuguese Prego With Piri-Piri

Preparation time: 15 minutes
Cook time: 8 minutes
Nutrition facts (per serving): 636 cal (30g fat, 42.8g protein, 4g fiber)

When you can't think of anything to serve for lunch or dinner, then this Prego with Piri-Piri will help you big time.

Ingredients (2 servings)
1 garlic clove, crushed
2 small rump steaks
2 tablespoons olive oil
1 tablespoon sherry vinegar
2 ciabatta rolls, toasted
2 handfuls rocket or arugula

Green Piri-Piri Sauce
1 small handful of basil leaves
1 small handful parsley leaves
1 jalapeño, chopped
1 tablespoon sherry vinegar
2 spring onions, chopped
½ garlic clove, chopped
½ teaspoons caster sugar

Preparation
Rub the steaks with garlic and place them in a sandwich bag. Add the sherry vinegar, olive oil, and parsley to the steaks. Seal the bag and mix the steak with the marinade by pressing everything with a rolling pin. Leave for 2 hours for marinating. Meanwhile, blend all the ingredients for the sauce with 1 tablespoon water in a blender until smooth. Sear the steaks with a

skillet greased with oil and sear them for 2 minutes per side. Transfer the cooked prego steaks to a plate and serve them with green sauce. Enjoy.

Grilled Portuguese Sardines

Preparation time: 10 minutes
Cook time: 10 minutes
Nutrition facts (per serving): 231 cal (14g fat, 26g protein, 1.1g fiber)

Here's another classic sardines recipe for your dinner or lunch recipe collection. Serve it with a tangy side salad and enjoy the best of it.

Ingredients (8 servings)
2 tablespoons olive oil
3 garlic cloves, sliced
1 tablespoon smoked sweet paprika
½ lemon, zested and wedged
4 rosemary sprigs, leaves stripped
1 red chili, deseeded and chopped
8 sardines, gutted

Preparation
Mix the olive oil, garlic, paprika, lemon zest, rosemary, and red chili in a bowl. Place the sardines on a baking sheet and rub the prepared marinade on top. Cover and refrigerate for 1 hour. Meanwhile, prepare and preheat the grill pan over medium heat. Sear the sardines for 5 minutes per side. Garnish with lemon wedges, paprika, and oil. Serve warm.

Piri-Piri Chicken with Winter Slaw

Preparation time: 10 minutes
Cook time: 1 hour 40 minutes
Nutrition facts (per serving): 418 cal (27g fat, 33g protein, 2.2g fiber)

Try this super tasty Portuguese Piri-Piri chicken for all your festive meal and you'll never stop having it; that's how heavenly the combination tastes.

Ingredients (6 servings)
3 ⅓ lbs. whole chicken

Piri-Piri Marinade
3 red chilies, chopped
2 garlic cloves, chopped
3cm ginger piece, chopped
1 teaspoon dried oregano
1 teaspoon ground coriander
1 teaspoon paprika
2 tablespoons red wine vinegar
2 tablespoons groundnut oil

Winter Slaw
1 red onion, sliced
2 carrots, peeled and shredded
1 beetroot, peeled and shredded
4 baby spinach leaf, shredded
2 tablespoons mayonnaise
2 tablespoons Greek yogurt
2 teaspoons red wine vinegar
1 teaspoon cumin seeds, seeded

Preparation
Blend all the Piri-Piri marinade ingredients in a blender for 1 minute and then rub it over the chicken. Leave the chicken for 1 hour. At 350 degrees F, preheat your oven. Place the prepared whole chicken in a roasting pan and bake for 1 hour and 20 minutes. Allow the chicken to cool for 20 minutes and mix all the ingredients for the slaw in a bowl. Serve the chicken with the slaw.

Desserts

Portuguese Sweet Rice

Preparation time: 15 minutes
Cook time: 60 minutes
Nutrition facts (per serving): 296 cal (5g fat, 9.5g protein, 3g fiber)

Here's a delicious and savory combination of rice and rice that you must add to your menu. It's truly one of the easiest Portuguese desserts.

Ingredients (4 servings)
1½ quarts milk
1 cup white rice
1 cup white sugar
2 eggs, beaten

Preparations
Mix the milk with sugar in a large saucepan over high heat until it bubbles. Add the rice and cook for 60 minutes on medium-low heat, then remove it from the heat. Stir in the beaten eggs, and then mix the rice vigorously. Serve warm.

Portuguese Muffins (*Bolo Levedo*)

Preparation time: 5 minutes
Cook time: 20 minutes
Nutrition facts (per serving): 287 cal (5g fat, 7.3g protein, 3g fiber)

These muffins are a typical Portuguese side meal, which is a must to have on the Portuguese menu. They're soft, moist, and fluffy.

Ingredients (12 servings)
1 (¼ ounce) envelope active dry yeast
¼ cup of warm water
6 cups all-purpose flour
1 cup white sugar
3 eggs
¼ cup melted butter cooled
½ teaspoon salt
1 ¼ cups milk

Preparation
Mix the warm water with yeast and sugar in a large suitable bowl and leave it for 10 minutes. Stir in the flour, milk, salt, eggs and then mix until the ingredients come together as dough. Knead the dough for 10 minutes. Cover the prepared dough with a plastic sheet and leave it for 1 hour. Punch the dough down and cut it into 20 pieces. Spread each dough piece into ½ inch thick round. Place the rounds in a baking sheet lined with parchment paper. Cover them with a kitchen towel and leave it for 1 ½ hour. Add oil to a deep cooking pan and heat to 350 degrees F. Fry the cakes until golden brown. Transfer to a plate lined with a paper towel. Serve.

Portuguese Coconut Cakes (*Bolos de Coco*)

Preparation time: 10 minutes
Cook time: 20 minutes
Nutrition facts (per serving): 624 cal (40g fat, 10g protein, 2g fiber)

Portuguese coconut cakes are here to add flavors to your dessert table. This effortless recipe gives you simple, tasty, and sweet coconut balls.

Ingredients (3 servings)
1 ¾ cups coconut, shredded
¾ cup white sugar
3 eggs
1 tablespoon lemon zest, grated

Preparation
At 350 degrees F, preheat your oven. Layer 3 muffin cups with paper cups. Mix the lemon zest, eggs, sugar, and coconut in a bowl. Divide the coconut mixture into the muffin cups. Bake them for 20 minutes in the oven. Serve.

Portuguese Custard Tarts (*Pasteis de Nata*)

Preparation time: 10 minutes
Cook time: 12 minutes
Nutrition facts (per serving): 210 cal (11g fat, 3.9g protein, 3g fiber)

If you haven't tried the Portuguese custard tarts before, then here comes an authentic, simple, and easy to cook recipe that you can recreate easily in minimum time.

Ingredients (12 servings)
Dough
1 cup all-purpose flour
¼ teaspoon salt
⅓ cup of cold water
1 stick unsalted butter, fully softened

Sugar Syrup
¾ cup white sugar
¼ cup of water
1 tablespoon water
1 cinnamon stick
1 lemon, zested

Custard Base
⅓ cup all-purpose flour
¼ teaspoon salt
1 ½ cups milk
6 large egg yolks
1 teaspoon vanilla extract

Preparation

Mix the all-purpose flour, salt, and cold water in a bowl until they come together as a dough. Knead the dough for 2 minutes, then cover and leave it for 20 minutes. Roll this dough into a ⅛-inch-thick square sheet and spread ⅓ butter over the square while leaving ½ inch border. Fold the edges over the buttered portion. Dust the prepared dough with flour, fold the dough, and again spread into a ⅛-inch-thick sheet, and repeat the layering. Place the sheet in a baking sheet and refrigerate for 10 minutes. Cut the dough into 12 rounds using a cookie cutter.

Mix the lemon zest, cinnamon, sugar, and ¼ cup 1 tablespoon water in a pot. Cook the mixture to a boil, and then remove it from the heat. Grease a 12-cup muffin pan. Divide the prepared dough into 12 pieces and layer one piece in each muffin cup. At 550 degrees, preheat your oven. Prepare the custard and mix the cold milk with salt and flour in a suitable saucepan, then cook until it thickens. Then remove it from the heat then allow it to cool. Add the egg yolks to the mixture and mix well. Stir in the vanilla extract and sugar syrup, and then mix well. Strain the custard through a sieve, then divide into the crust, then bake for 12 minutes.

Serradura

Preparation time: 15 minutes
Nutrition facts (per serving): 347 cal (5g fat, 7g protein, 5g fiber)

A dessert that has no parallel, the Portuguese Serradura is made with layers of biscuits and cream.

Ingredients (2 servings)
1 cup heavy whipping cream
¼ cup sweetened condensed milk
18 Marie Biscuits
½ teaspoon pure vanilla extract
Chocolate shavings, strawberries, or mint for garnish

Preparation
Blend the biscuits in a blender to crush into crumbs. Beat the cream with vanilla in a suitable mixer until fluffy. Stir in the milk and beat until they make stiff peaks. Add a layer of biscuit crumbs in the serving glasses and then top with a cream mixture. Repeat 5-7 layers in the serving glasses. Garnish with chocolate shavings and strawberries. Refrigerate for 4 hours and then serve.

Portuguese Doughnuts (*Bola De Berlim*)

Preparation time: 15 minutes
Cook time: 40 minutes
Nutrition facts (per serving): 221 cal (3 g fat, 4 g protein, 2.8g fiber)

Yes, you can make something as delicious and simple as these doughnuts by using only basic dessert and cookie ingredients and some basic techniques.

Ingredients (12 servings)
2 sachets dried yeast
⅓ cup caster sugar, plus extra, to coat
½ cup lukewarm milk
3 eggs, beaten
2 ½ ounces unsalted butter, melted
17 ½ ounces plain flour
Vegetable oil, to deep-fry

Crème pâtissière
⅓ cup plain flour
⅓ cup caster sugar
1 egg
4 egg yolks
1½ cups milk
2 drops yellow food coloring

Preparation
Beat the egg yolks with egg, sugar, and flour in a bowl until creamy and pale. Boil ½ cup milk in a pan and stir in the flour mixture. Next, cook for 5 minutes with occasional stirring. Stir in a few drops of yellow color and mix well. Strain the mixture through a sieve into a bowl. Mix the remaining milk, ¼ cup water, sugar, and yeast in a suitable saucepan, and then cook for 10 minutes until it bubbles. Stir in the eggs and butter.

Mix the flour with sugar and yeast mixture in a bowl and mix well for 5 minutes until smooth. Knead the dough, transfer to a bowl, cover and leave it for 1 hour. Divide the prepared dough into 12 balls and place them on a baking sheet lined with flour and cover it with a plastic sheet, then leave it for 30 minutes. Heat the oil to 350 degrees F in a deep-frying pan and deep fry the doughnuts in the hot oil until golden brown. Transfer the doughnuts to a plate and cut them in half. Add the 2 ½ tablespoons crème pâtissière in between two halves of the doughnuts. Serve.

Flan

Preparation time: 15 minutes
Cook time: 55 minutes
Nutrition facts (per serving): 357 cal (12g fat, 5.5g protein, 1.4g fiber)

Try this flan on the Portuguese menu. The sweet combination of sugar, eggs, and vanilla is bliss for all the sweet tooth fans like me.

Ingredients (4 servings)
1 ½ cups sugar
2 tablespoons water
½ lemon, juiced
2 cups double cream
1 cinnamon stick
1 vanilla bean, split
3 large eggs
2 large egg yolks
1 pinch salt

Preparation
Mix 1 cup sugar with 2 tablespoons water in a suitable saucepan and cook for 10 minutes while stirring until caramelized. Remove this prepared mixture from the heat and stir in lemon juice. Mix and pour this prepared mixture into a flan mold. At 350 degrees F, preheat your oven. Boil water in a suitable saucepan and keep it warm in a large baking pan.

Mix the cream with vanilla and cinnamon in a suitable saucepan and cook over medium-low heat until it boils. Beat the eggs with the egg yolks, 1 pinch salt, and ½ cup sugar in a bowl until creamy and thick. Pass this prepared mixture through a strainer. Pour this prepared mixture into the flan mold and place it in the water bath. Bake the flan for 45 minutes, and then allow it to cool. Refrigerate for 4 hours and then flip the flan over the serving plate. Serve.

Portuguese Bread (*Pão De Deus*)

Preparation time: 10 minutes
Cook time: 30 minutes
Nutrition facts (per serving): 425 cal (17g fat, 5g protein, 0.8g fiber)

This Portuguese bread will leave you spellbound due to its mildly sweet taste and the combination of crispy coconut topping over soft bread.

Ingredients (8 servings)
Dough
½ cup warm milk
⅓ cup water
1 tablespoon dry yeast
2 eggs
1 tablespoon rum
1 teaspoon vanilla extract
1 tablespoon lemon zest
3 ½ cups all-purpose flour
¼ cup 2 tablespoons sugar
¼ cup butter
½ teaspoon salt

Coconut crust
2 cups coconut, grated
½ cup 1 tablespoon sugar
1 egg
To Brush
1 beaten egg for brushing
Icing sugar

Preparation

For the crust, mix the coconut with sugar and 1 egg in a bowl. Prepare the dough and mix the warm milk, water, yeast, and sugar in a large suitable bowl. Leave it for 5 minutes. Beat the eggs with rum, lemon zest, ¼ cup sugar, and vanilla extract in another bowl. Stir in the flour, salt, remaining sugar, and the yeast mixture. Mix well until it makes smooth dough. Add butter and knead the dough to incorporate it. Place the dough in a greased bowl, cover with a plastic sheet and leave it for 1 hour. Divide the prepared dough into 10 buns, place them on a baking sheet, brush them with the beaten egg, and top each bun with coconut crust mixture. Bake the buns for 30 minutes, then garnish with icing sugar. Serve.

Almond Carob Cake
(*Tarte De Alfarroba E Amendôas*)

Preparation time: 15 minutes
Cook time: 40 minutes
Nutrition facts (per serving): 169 cal (12g fat, 8g protein, 4g fiber)

The famous Portuguese carob cake is essential to try on the Portuguese dessert menu. Try cooking it at home with these healthy ingredients and enjoy it.

Ingredients (6 servings)
1 cup flour
1 cup of sugar
1 tablespoon honey
1 cup carob powder
½ cup of oatmeal
3 tablespoons olive oil
½ cup almonds, chopped
1 cup milk
4 eggs
1 tablespoon baking powder
1 tablespoon confectioners' sugar

Preparation
At 355 degrees F, preheat your oven. Beat the egg whites in a bowl until creamy. Mix the oatmeal, flour, sugar, honey carob powder, and baking powder in a bowl until smooth. Stir in the milk, almond, oil, and beaten egg yolks. Mix well until smooth, and then gently fold in egg whites. Spread the prepared batter in a greased baking pan and bake for 40 minutes. Allow the cake to cool, then garnish with sugar. Slice and serve.

Egg White Soufflé (*Pudim Molotof*)

Preparation time: 10 minutes
Cook time: 12 minutes
Nutrition facts (per serving): 408 cal (20g fat, 34g protein, 0.4g fiber)

If you want something exotic on your dinner table, then nothing can taste better than this delicious egg white soufflé.

Ingredients (4 servings)
12 egg whites
2 cups of sugar
Caramel sauce
2 cups of sugar
1 tablespoon water

Preparation
Layer a large Bundt pan with oil. Prepare the caramel sauce in a skillet and cook until caramelized. Pour 3 tablespoons of sugar mixture into the Bundt pan and keep it aside. Beat the egg whites with sugar and 3 tablespoons remaining caramel sauce in a suitable mixer until it makes stiff peaks. Add the egg to the pan and bake for 12 minutes at 375 degrees F in the oven. Flip the pan over the serving plate and serve.

Orange Roll Cake

Preparation time: 10 minutes
Cook time: 14 minutes
Nutrition facts (per serving): 202 cal (7g fat, 6g protein, 1.3g fiber)

If you love citrus flavored cakes, then this Portuguese orange roll cake recipe is the right fit for you. Try this at home and cook in no time.

Ingredients (6 servings)
4 eggs yolks
4 egg whites
½ cup granulated sugar
¾ cup all-purpose flour
Juice of one orange
Zest of one orange
Sugar for dusting
1 teaspoon baking powder
¼ cup margarine

Preparation
Beat 4 egg whites in a suitable mixer until fluffy. Next, beat the egg yolks with orange zest and granulated sugar in another bowl until fluffy. Stir in the orange juice and zest. Mix well, and then add the flour, baking powder, and margarine then mix until smooth. Fold in the egg whites, then spread the batter in a 14 ¼ x 11 ¾ inches baking pan, lined with parchment paper and butter. Bake the batter for 14 minutes at 350 degrees F. Allow the cake to cool and transfer to a working surface. Finally, drizzle sugar on top, then roll the cake. Slice and serve.

Brigadeiro Cake

Preparation time: 10 minutes
Cook time: 71 minutes
Nutrition facts (per serving): 330 cal (13g g fat, 7.5g protein, 2g fiber)

The famous Portuguese brigadeiro cake is another special dessert to try on the Portuguese menu. Replicate at home with these healthy ingredients and enjoy it.

Ingredients (8 servings)
Cake
5 ⅓ ounces dark chocolate
¼ cup milk
Zest of one lemon
5 egg yolks
5 egg whites
1 cup dark brown sugar
¼ cup margarine
1 cup all-purpose flour
1 teaspoon baking powder

Filling
1 cup chocolate powder
1 cup milk
14 ounces condensed milk
Chocolate sprinkles, to taste

Preparation
At 350 degrees F, preheat your oven. Grease a cake pan with margarine and flour. Beat 5 egg whites in a suitable mixer until fluffy. Melt the chocolate with margarine in a bowl by heating it in the microwave for 1 minute. Mix well and keep it aside. Beat the egg yolks with sugar and milk in a bowl. Stir

in the chocolate mixture. Fold in the flour and baking powder, and then mix well until smooth. Fold in the egg whites, mix, and spread the batter in the pan. Bake for 45 minutes. Meanwhile, mix the milk, condensed milk, and chocolate powder in a pan over low heat and cook for 25 minutes until it thickens. Allow the cake and the filling to cool. Slice the cake in half horizontally. Place one cake half on the serving plate, top it with ½ of the filling, and place the other half of the baked cake on top. Spread the remaining filling on top. Garnish with chocolate sprinkles. Slice and serve.

Chocolate Mousse

Preparation time: 15 minutes
Cook time: 1 minute
Nutrition facts (per serving): 327 cal (18g fat, 7g protein, 2.6g fiber)

This chocolate mousse has no parallel; this simple mousse recipe has a delicious blend of dark chocolate, egg, and sugar.

Ingredients (6 servings)
½ cup granulated sugar
5 eggs
7 ounces dark chocolate
2 tablespoons margarine

Preparation
Add the chocolate chunks and butter to a bowl and melt them by heating them in the microwave for 1 minute. Mix well until it's creamy. Beat the egg whites in a bowl until fluffy. Beat the egg yolks with sugar in a mixer until creamy. Stir in the melted chocolate and mix well. Fold in the egg whites and mix. Divide the prepared mixture into the serving bowls and refrigerate for 4 hours. Garnish and serve.

Portuguese Almond Cake (*Toucinho Do Céu*)

Preparation time: 10 minutes
Cook time: 32 minutes
Nutrition facts (per serving): 203 cal (7g fat, 3g protein, 1g fiber)

The Portuguese almond cake is great to serve with all the hot beverages, and it's popular for its prominently sweet and earthy taste.

Ingredients (8 servings)
½ cup water
1 ¼ cups sugar
⅛ teaspoon salt
1 ¾ cups ground almonds, skinless
4 tablespoons unsalted butter
5 egg yolks
2 whole eggs
1 teaspoon almond extract
1 teaspoon orange zest, grated
All-purpose flour, for dusting
2 tablespoons pork lard

Preparation
At 325 degrees F, preheat your oven. Layer a cake pan with parchment paper and grease it with butter. Boil the water with pork lard, salt, and sugar in a suitable saucepan, and then stir in ground almonds. Mix well and cook on medium-low heat for 2 minutes until the mixture thickens. Remove the pan from the heat, then add butter and mix well. Beat the eggs with yolks in a bowl. Stir in the almond butter, orange zest, and amaretto, and then mix well. Spread the batter in the prepared pan and bake for 30 minutes. Allow the cake to cool. Slice and serve.

Chocolate Salami (*Salame De Chocolate*)

Preparation time: 10 minutes
Cook time: 10 minutes
Nutrition facts (per serving): 58 cal (1.4g fat, 1g protein, 2g fiber)

This Portuguese chocolate salami is worth the try as it tastes so unique and exotic. This dessert is definitely a must on the Portuguese menu.

Ingredients (6 servings)
7 ounces dark chocolate
3 ounces unsalted butter
⅓ cup sugar
2 eggs
7 ounces Maria biscuits, crushed
½ teaspoon vanilla extract
2 tablespoons powdered sugar

Preparation
Boil water in a suitable saucepan and place a glass bowl over the water. Add the butter and chocolate to the bowl and cook until melted. Beat the sugar with vanilla extract and eggs in another bowl. Stir in the chocolate melts and mix well. Stir in the biscuit pieces, mix and leave it for 10 minutes. Spread the prepared mixture in a loaf pan lined with parchment paper. Allow the log to cool, slice, garnish with sugar, and serve.

Portuguese Vermicelli Pudding (Aletria)

Preparation time: 15 minutes
Cook time: 20 minutes
Nutrition facts (per serving): 289 cal (13g fat, 3g protein, 2g fiber)

If you haven't tried the Portuguese Aletria before, then here comes an authentic, simple, and easy to cook recipe that you can recreate easily at home in minimum time.

Ingredients (6 servings)
5 ⅓ rice vermicelli noodles
2 ½ cup rice milk
2 egg yolks
½ cup granulated sugar
1 pinch of salt
1 tablespoon butter
1 big lemon peel
1 cinnamon stick
Ground cinnamon for dusting

Preparation
Beat the egg yolks with ½ cup milk in a bowl. Mix the milk with a cinnamon stick, lemon peel, butter, salt, sugar, and water in a suitable saucepan, and then cook for 5 minutes. Discard the lemon peel and cinnamon stick. Boil the remaining mixture, then add vermicelli noodles and cook for 10 minutes. Remove the prepared pudding from the heat and slowly pour in the egg-yolk mixture. Mix well and garnish with cinnamon. Serve.

Drunken Pears

Preparation time: 15 minutes
Cook time: 55 minutes
Nutrition facts (per serving): 650 cal (36g fat, 12g protein, 0g fiber)

The famous drunken pears are essential to try on the Portuguese dessert menu. Try cooking them at home with these healthy ingredients and enjoy.

Ingredients (8 servings)
4 medium ripe pears, peeled
½ lemon, zest, and juice
1 ½ cups red wine
4 ½ ounces brown sugar
2 cinnamon sticks
¼ cup Port wine

Preparation
Add the cinnamon sticks, red wine, brown sugar, lemon zest, and juice to a saucepan. Toss in pears and cook for 15 minutes. Transfer the pears to a plate. Pour the port wine into the pan and cook for 40 minutes on low heat. Serve with pears and the sauce on top.

Pumpkin Dreams (*Sonhos de Abóbora*)

Preparation time: 15 minutes
Cook time: 10 minutes
Nutrition facts (per serving): 228 cal (6g fat, 4g protein, 3g fiber)

Pumpkin dream is one good option to go for in the desserts. You can also keep them ready and stored, but then use them instead as instant desserts.

Ingredients (12 servings)
1 cup milk
1 cup of water
8 tablespoons vegetable oil
1 pinch of salt
1 lemon or orange zest
1 ¼ cups flour
9 ounces pumpkin purée
4 eggs
Cinnamon and sugar, for serving

Preparation
Mix all the ingredients, including the flour and milk, in a mixing bowl of a mixer until it makes a smooth dough. Divide the prepared dough into 2 teaspoons of oval-shaped pieces. Deep fry the ovals in a wok filled with hot oil until golden brown. Transfer the ovals to a plate lined with a paper towel. Drizzle cinnamon and sugar on top. Serve.

Washboard Cookies (*Lavadores*)

Preparation time: 10 minutes
Cook time: 30 minutes
Nutrition facts (per serving): 186 cal (12g fat, 4g protein, 2.5g fiber)

Without these washboard cookies, it seems like the Portuguese dessert menu is incomplete. Try them with different variations of toppings.

Ingredients (12 servings)
½ cup butter
1 cup of sugar
4 eggs
Zest of a 1 lemon
4 cups flour
1 tablespoon baking powder
⅛ teaspoon salt
¼ cup sugar

Preparation
At 350 degrees F, preheat your oven. Blend 1 cup sugar with butter in a suitable mixer until creamy. Next, add the eggs while beating the mixture until pale yellow and fluffy. Stir in the lemon zest and mix well. Stir in the flour, baking powder, and salt, then mix well for 5 minutes. Knead this dough for 5 minutes. Divide the prepared dough into 3 inches balls and coat them with sugar. Place the balls on a greased baking sheet and bake for 20 minutes. Serve once cooled.

Portuguese Almond Cupcakes

Preparation time: 10 minutes
Cook time: 25 minutes
Nutrition facts (per serving): 141 cal (4g fat, 2g protein, 1.1g fiber)

Here comes a dessert that is most loved by all. The almond cupcakes aren't only served as a dessert, but also as a famous street food.

Ingredients (12 servings)
½ cup of water
2 egg yolks
3 eggs
2 ounces of almonds, chopped
1 cup of flour
¾ cup of sugar
1 cupcake baking sheet
¼ cup of almonds, chopped
1 tablespoon of powdered sugar
12 cupcake baking papers

Preparation
At 375 degrees F, preheat your oven. Mix the sugar with water in a suitable saucepan over medium heat and cook it to a boil. Beat the eggs, yolks, and 2 ounces almonds in a bowl. Add this prepared mixture to the saucepan and mix well until smooth. Divide this batter into a greased cupcake pan and bake for 25 minutes in the oven. Garnish with chopped almond and powdered sugar. Serve.

Drinks

Caprioska Cocktail

Preparation time: 5 minutes
Nutrition facts (per serving): 112 cal (0g fat, 1g protein, 3g fiber)

Beat the heat and try the famous Portuguese Caprioska cocktail with the hints of lime and crushed ice. The combination is super refreshing and healthy.

Ingredients (1 serving)
½ lime, quartered
1 tablespoon white sugar
1 ½ ounces vodka
Crushed ice

Preparation
Add white sugar and vodka to a cocktail shaker. Mix well and pour into a glass filled with ice. Garnish with lime quarters. Serve.

Porto Tonico

Preparation time: 5 minutes
Nutrition facts (per serving): 103cal (0g fat, 1g protein, 1g fiber)

The Portuguese Porto Tonico is loved due to its refreshing taste and sweet flavors. Serve chilled for the best taste and flavor.

Ingredients (1 serving)
1 ½ ounce white port
3 ounces tonic
1 fresh mint sprig
1 orange wedge
Ice cubes

Preparation
Add the white port, tonic, and mint sprig to a pitcher. Mix well and add an orange wedge. Serve with ice cubes.

Portuguese Daisy

Preparation time: 10 minutes
Nutrition facts (per serving): 117 cal (0g fat, 1g protein, 0g fiber)

The Portuguese daisy drink is great to serve on any special occasions or memorable dinner. It has this appealing mix of simple syrup with lemon juice and brandy.

Ingredients (2 servings)
2 ounces port wine
1-ounce brandy
1-ounce lemon juice
1 teaspoon simple syrup
1 teaspoon grenadine

Preparation
Add the port wine, brandy, lemon juice, simple syrup, and grenadine to a cocktail shaker. Next, shake well. Serve.

Sour Cherry Liqueur (*Ginginha*)

Preparation time: 10 minutes
Cook time: 5 minutes
Nutrition facts (per serving): 142 cal (1g fat, 6.3g protein, 1g fiber)

The Portuguese sour cherry liqueur is famous for its blend of cherries, brandy, and red wine. You can ready this drink easily at home.

Ingredients (4 servings)
2 cups sour cherries
1 ¼ cups Portuguese Brandy
½ cup red wine
1 cinnamon stick
2 cloves
2 cups brown sugar

Preparation
Add sugar and red wine to a saucepan and cook on medium heat. Then cook on low heat for 5 minutes. Allow the wine to cool, and then divide it into 4 medium mason jars. Add the cherries, cloves, cinnamon sticks, and Portuguese Brandy. Seal the lid and place the jars in a dark place for 1 month. Remove the cloves and cinnamon and then serve the wine with the cherries. Enjoy.

Portonic

Preparation time: 5 minutes
Nutrition facts (per serving): 156 cal (0g fat, 0.7g protein, 1.4g fiber)

The Portonic is all that you need to celebrate the holidays. Keep the drink ready in your refrigerator for quick serving.

Ingredients (1 serving)
2 ounces white port
1 dash of lime juice
Ice
2 ounces tonic water
Grapes to garnish

Preparation
Add the white port, lime juice, and tonic water to a cocktail shaker. Shake well and serve with ice and grapes. Enjoy.

Portuguese Martini

Preparation time: 5 minutes
Nutrition facts (per serving): 114 cal (0g fat, 0g protein, 0.3g fiber)

Here's a special Portuguese drink, which is great to serve at special dinners and celebrations.

Ingredients (1 serving)
3 ounces Martini sweet, dry vermouth
A splash of gin
Lemon slices, for garnish

Preparation
Add the martini sweet, dry vermouth and gin to a cocktail shaker. Next, shake well. Garnish with lemon slices. Serve.

Portuguese Morangao Cocktail

Preparation time: 5 minutes
Nutrition facts (per serving): 110 cal (0g fat, 0g protein, 1g fiber)

Here's a Portuguese Morangao cocktail made from strawberries and lime juice, which is great to serve at special dinners and festive celebrations.

Ingredients (2 servings)
1 cup strawberries
Juice from 1 Lime
Crushed ice
Licor Beirão, to serve

Preparation
Blend the strawberries with lemon juice and crushed ice in a blender. Serve with Licor Beirão.

Vinho Verde Sangria

Preparation time: 5 minutes
Nutrition facts (per serving): 112 cal (0g fat, 1g protein, 2.3g fiber)

It's a Portuguese drink made out of refreshing peaches, apples, and grapes, which is perfect to serve at special dinners and memorable celebrations.

Ingredients (4 servings)
2 peaches, cubed
1 apple, cubed
½-pound green grapes, sliced
2 (750 ml) bottles Vinho Verde
1 cup triple sec

Preparation
Mix the peaches with apple, green grapes, Vinho Verde, and triple sec in a pitcher. Serve.

If you liked Portuguese recipes, discover to how cook DELICIOUS recipes from **Balkan** countries!

Within these pages, you'll learn 35 authentic recipes from a Balkan cook. These aren't ordinary recipes you'd find on the Internet, but recipes that were closely guarded by our Balkan mothers and passed down from generation to generation.

Main Dishes, Appetizers, and Desserts included!

If you want to learn how to make Croatian green peas stew, and 32 other authentic Balkan recipes, then start with our book!

Order at www.balkanfood.org/cook-books/ for only $2,99

If you're a **Mediterranean** dieter who wants to know the secrets of the Mediterranean diet, dieting, and cooking, then you're about to discover how to master cooking meals on a Mediterranean diet right now!

In fact, if you want to know how to make Mediterranean food, then this new e-book - "The 30-minute Mediterranean diet" - gives you the answers to many important questions and challenges every Mediterranean dieter faces, including:
- How can I succeed with a Mediterranean diet?
- What kind of recipes can I make?
- What are the key principles to this type of diet?
- What are the suggested weekly menus for this diet?
- Are there any cheat items I can make?

... and more!

If you're serious about cooking meals on a Mediterranean diet and you really want to know how to make Mediterranean food, then you need to grab a copy of "The 30-minute Mediterranean diet" right now.
Prepare **111 recipes with several ingredients in less than 30 minutes**!

Order at www.balkanfood.org/cook-books/ for only $2,99

What could be better than a home-cooked meal? Maybe only a **Greek** homemade meal.

Do not get discouraged if you have no Greek roots or friends. Now you can make a Greek food feast in your kitchen.

This ultimate Greek cookbook offers you 111 best dishes of this cuisine! From more famous gyros to more exotic *Kota Kapama* this cookbook keeps it easy and affordable.

All the ingredients necessary are wholesome and widely accessible. The author's picks are as flavorful as they are healthy. The dishes described in this cookbook are "what Greek mothers have made for decades."

Full of well-balanced and nutritious meals, this handy cookbook includes many vegan options. Discover a plethora of benefits of Mediterranean cuisine, and you may fall in love with cooking at home.

Inspired by a real food lover, this collection of delicious recipes will taste buds utterly satisfied.

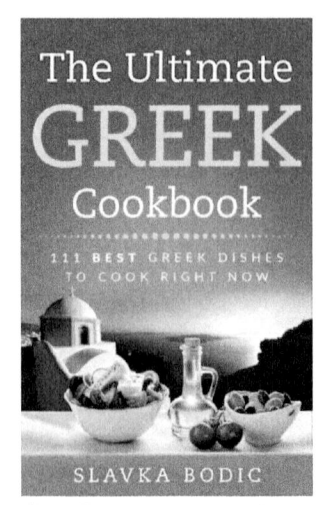

Order at www.balkanfood.org/cook-books/ for only $2,99

Maybe to try exotic **Syrian** cuisine?

From succulent *sarma*, soups, warm and cold salads to delectable desserts, the plethora of flavors will satisfy the most jaded foodie. Have a taste of a new culture with this **traditional Syrian cookbook**.

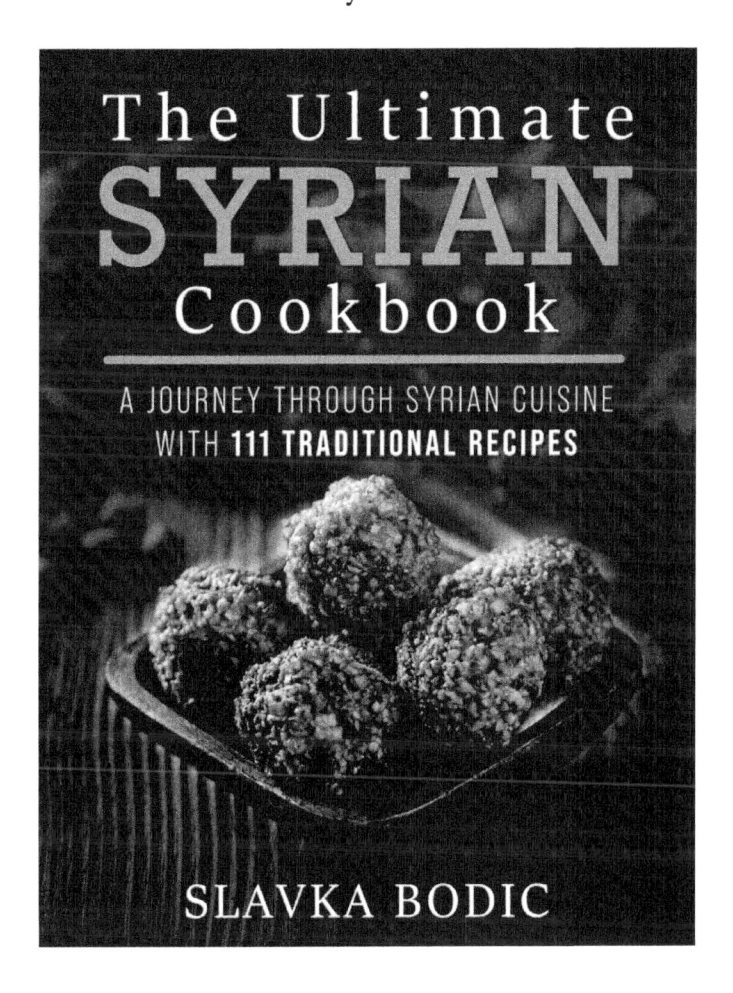

Order at www.balkanfood.org/cook-books/ for only $2,99

Maybe **Polish** cuisine?

Order at www.balkanfood.org/cook-books/ for only $2,99

ONE LAST THING

If you enjoyed this book or found it useful, I'd be very grateful if you could find the time to post a short review on Amazon. Your support really does make a difference and I read all the reviews personally, so I can get your feedback and make this book even better.

Thanks again for your support!

Please send me your feedback at

www.balkanfood.org

Printed in Great Britain
by Amazon